THE THIRD OPTION

....

*In a World of Codependency
with Only Two Choices*

John,
God Bless
Steve Horne
Rom 8:38-39

By Steve Horne

HERITAGE BUILDERS PUBLISHING

RIO VISTA, CALIFORNIA; TROY, ALABAMA;
MANAGUA, NICARAGUA; NASHVILLE, TENNESSEE

HERITAGE BUILDERS PUBLISHING

THE THIRD OPTION
In a World of Codependency with Only Two Choices

Copyright © 2019 by Steve Horne

First Edition 2019

Cover Design: Rae House
Editing and Book Design: Nord Compo

Published by Heritage Builders Publishing
Rio Vista, California
Troy, Alabama
Managua, Nicaragua
Nashville, Tennesse

www.HeritageBuildersPublishing.com
1-800-397-8267
ISBN: 978-1-94554925-0

Printed and Bound in the USA

Table of Contents

STATEMENT

This book is written for:

- The person who wants to understand codependency, and its potential to steal, kill, and destroy.

- The person who already understands codependency, and wants to continue growing and healing from its effects.

- The person who cannot tell you what codependency is, or if they have it.

- The person who thinks codependency is an overused term, but fails to see its influence everywhere.

DEDICATION

Above my desk, on the wall behind the computer monitor, is a list of names with the title "Why I Write." In one section are the names of parents whose children who are no longer with us, those whose lives were taken by addiction. The parents and children's names are listed side by side; my wife Sharon and I are included in this list. In the other section are the names of people I have personally worked with, whose children have struggled with addiction, but their son or daughter is still alive. Their names are listed side by side as well. Regardless of which list they are on, all have suffered. It reminds me of why I do what I do; it keeps me focused on what really matters. Until there is no list, it is "Why I Write."

This book is dedicated to my list, and to yours.

ACKNOWLEDGMENTS

Few people better understand the sacrifices that go along with helping people than the spouses of those who minister. I would like to thank my wife Sharon for her continued support, love, and commitment to "our" ministry. I could not do what I do without her.

To the people that God used to speak truth into my life, even when I did not want to hear it. My personal journey with codependency started over 25 years ago, and continues to this day.

To the people who have had the courage to call and ask for help. Through the many experiences of helping people with their own codependency, I have learned much about the depths of this subject. A great deal of the knowledge and solutions that are contained in this book came from helping other people, even when they did not want to hear it.

To the people who do not have the courage to call or ask for help. Whatever the reason might be, doing nothing is a choice. May God bless your decision to read this book, even if you really do not want to.

I would like to also acknowledge those who were contributing editors, whose help and expertise were invaluable towards the quality of the book, as well as making sure the concepts and illustrations worked to communicate the message. A special thank you to Donna Hunt, Zachary Horner, and Maggie Yow for their contributions.

CLARIFICATION

There is a pattern throughout this book with the use of "italics" and "quotation" marks to clarify the origin and sources of information. Three combinations of these are consistently used:

1. Bible Scriptures are noted with italics and quotation marks, as well as the book, chapter, and verse listed.
2. Comments that are the author's original statements are noted with italics and quotations without any additional reference.
3. General quotes of interest are noted with quotation marks, but without italics. These are from both known and unknown sources, or shown as a quote from conversations. Others are parts of a Scripture where the idea is being referenced without quoting the complete verse.

Another pattern throughout the book is to use real life testimonies, but protect the identity of the person by changing the name to a generic one combined with a number, such as Ruth E. #1 and Ron E. #1. The pattern continues throughout the book with only the number changing.

A TESTIMONY FROM THE AUTHOR

....

A s I was working through the bibliography for this book, I recalled a series of events that took place in 1999 that God used to open doors for our ministry, and show me what was to come. These events are the origin of chapter three in this book on the subject of abandonment.

That year a small group of people including myself organized a recovery conference at our home church (Napa Valley Baptist Church, Napa, CA). It was a one-day event with several speakers, basic and simple. We had people there from out of town because of the focus on Christian Recovery. I wrote the message on abandonment and gave the presentation at this conference. One of the people from out of town was so impacted by the message that I was invited to give the same presentation at a large event in Chicago later that same year.

In the fall of 1999 my wife Sharon and I traveled to Chicago. Up until that point the largest crowd I had ever spoken in front of was about 200. There were just fewer than 1,000 people at this event, including some well-known authors such as Steve Arterburn, Brennan Manning, and others. Upon arriving I found out that the person who asked me to come had scheduled me to speak in a general session for the conference, where everyone would be in the auditorium. Brennan Manning was the keynote speaker the evening before I gave my presentation. It was a great event and challenged me personally to be in front of a crowd that size and with the level of experience, which was present. I had only been writing my own material for one year at that time, and this was just the second message I had developed.

I was nervous and had prayed the night before so I could surrender the whole experience to the Lord. Even so, it was challenging to get started with so many people in such a huge building (capacity for 2500). About 10 minutes into the message I realized that I was still standing behind the podium, speaking my way through the power point slides. That was not my way of teaching, and I knew it. That first step out felt like a big one, but that's when God moved. Talking with Sharon later she said I had talked for 10 minutes then stepped out and became myself. For the next hour I delivered the message, and experienced what it's like when God really takes over and the passion comes through.

After finishing I stepped down from the podium, and that was as far as I got. I was engulfed in people, some were in tears, others to say thanks, most just had this look of amazement for what they had received. God had really done something with the message, and I remained there for at least 30 minutes speaking with people and answering questions. Sharon was right there as well experiencing the moment. One lady was almost begging to know if I had any resources, materials, or books. At that time I had none, so it bothered me to say "no." Afterward is when we started recording and reproducing my messages. Then a woman confronted me and wanted to know if I realized that I had contradicted Brennan Manning from his message the previous evening. I told her politely that he was entitled to his opinion, but he was wrong. Several other people close by looked surprised by that comment. One statement I heard several times was people saying how they had never heard the subject explained like that before. One person asked how long it took to write it message, I said "a lifetime" because it was all based on my personal experience. Some wanted to know where I had studied, UHK was my answer, university of hard knocks. The person who invited me to speak watched all of this take place, and later said that is why she made the invitation, because her own recovery had involved a lot of work on abandonment issues including professional counseling, but she had never heard it explained they way that I did. It had laid to rest some of the issues that were still affecting her and was hoping the message would have the same impact on others. It did.

The same day that I gave that presentation, other speakers were already quoting and using points from the message in theirs, some as additions to the handouts they had already prepared. Later that night when we arrived at the hotel, a woman came up to us in the lobby and told me that I probably didn't realize how much of an impact that message had on people. I agreed, and gave credit to God for using it.

Several important things happened through these events:

- Doubts that I had about using my own experiences to develop teaching material were gone.
- I knew I had to put those experiences into tangible resources.
- No matter how accurate the information was, some people would want credentials.
- That God had given me an ability to explain life in a way that made sense to other people, even on subjects they were already familiar with.
- Just because someone is well known doesn't make them right, and I can use my experience to disagree and prove the truth, even if they are famous or have letters after their name.
- I learned that some of the materials I could develop would be used by other people, multiplying the ability to help others.

- And, that God wanted me to keep going, keep writing, and keep speaking, from experience. He has also provided more experiences to learn from.

That was almost 20 years ago, and the lessons learned from that event are still being used. Everywhere I've gone, in the US and several foreign countries, people's eyes are opened to the truth in a way they have never heard before, and someone always wants to know what my credentials are.

It will be interesting to see how this book is received, and if it holds to the pattern. If so, many people will find truth and healing, some will question the source, others will pick it up and use it in their ministries, and it will contradict a few experts. In any case, it will be successful as long as it helps people and honors God.

FOREWORD

S teve Horne's book, "The Third Option" is a must read for everyone! I am convinced that codependency is the thief of joy and real purpose in the lives of many people. The sad thing is many people do not know they are codependent. They think they are just helping to "fix" the problems in the lives of others, or have an honest desire to "help" in the midst of difficult circumstances. The true success of living is knowing our God given abilities, and setting boundaries to keep us from trying to control others for the purpose of bringing about our goals for their lives. Many leaders, even Religious Leaders, fall into the trap of functioning outside healthy boundaries and thus manifest their own codependency.

Then there are those who are the victims of the actions of the codependent. Many times these innocent victims do not identify the codependency that is controlling those other people who are affecting their lives. Steve's book will clarify the characteristics of the codependent, give help to those who are plagued with codependency, and help others understand the actions and character of the codependent.

Steve writes from years of experience of working with addicts and alcoholics, all of which he says suffer from codependency. His wealth of knowledge and plainspoken style will open the eyes, and hopefully the hearts of all who read his writings. Steve has also done research and much study on the subject of codependency. Writing from material that one has studied is good, but even better when the student also has "hands on experience." I recommend that you set aside a quiet time and read carefully "The Third Option." I only wish I had could have had a resource like this to guide me in my youth! God bless and enjoy Steve Horne's insight and instruction on this pressing subject for these days.

Dr Rudy Holland
1st Corinthians 10:13

PREFACE

There is a popular belief that codependents should be approached with extreme caution and tenderness, as not to hurt them since they are so fragile. This is true in the context of someone who has codependent tendencies, such as the parent of child who dies from addiction and finds out later that mistakes were made that were codependent in nature. There are also people who have not experienced the loss of a loved one, but they live in fear of the same outcome and make decisions that are codependent and unhealthy. Great injury could be caused by the wrong approach to addressing codependency for these people, or many others who simply need emotional and spiritual healing. However, to the person who is a passive/aggressive codependent, who causes pain and suffering in the lives of others and refuses to accept responsibility for their actions, no such approach should be used. These types of people need more of an intervention that is confrontational by nature. But how can we tell the difference?

Codependents are like "salsa." You can find it almost anywhere you go in various flavors, but it's still basically the same product. The differences are in the ingredients: some are mild or medium, while others are flaming hot. If you don't have experience in eating salsa, and the waiter at a restaurant brings more than one bowl, you might not know the difference between hot and mild unless someone tells you. Otherwise you could just test it out and possibly suffer for it, and the pain might last for a while. Salsa bought in a store is much easier to understand; it has labels that list the ingredients. Some show flames with the word "hot" written on it while others are labeled as medium or mild. If the label is written in a foreign language, you might have to look at the pictures and just hope for the best. But labels can be deceptive, or sometimes the wrong label could be covering up the true ingredients.

In a world of codependency, there are a lot of codependents running around with no labels. An inexperienced person might not find out whom they are dealing with until after a painful encounter. Even if you do know what they are made of, do you know enough to understand the differences between mild and hot? Some people appear to be good-natured and supportive until you have difficulty with them, and they vent like a volcano. People that have experience in dealing with codependency have a better chance of identifying it, and knowing when it's mild or hot. All of this would be made much easier if people had labels, and even though we might be inclined to say they do not, they actually do. The real issue is being able to read the label and know what it says about the ingredients on the inside. Yet, some people are masters at covering up the true ingredients with a false label.

In this book you will learn a lot about the problem of codependency as well as the solution, whether it is in your own life, the life of another person, or the world around you. We all have some type of codependent tendencies; it's what makes us human. You will learn about the warning signs and how to read them properly. Some of this is a journey inward, to the heart and soul of who you are. Other parts are a journey outward, to see people and circumstances in a different light. Ultimately the goal is not self-serving, it is about knowing God at a deeper level and being used by Him in a world that needs solutions.

Some of the basic principles for this book are similar to those from "*7 Things Christians Need to Know About Addiction*" by the same author, where the subject of recovery was addressed extensively. It is a good resource to understand the connection between the 12 Step Recovery Process and the Bible/Christianity. As such, the subject of recovery will be referred to in this book as a solution without re-establishing its origins or value.

One common theme between the two books that does need to be re-established is "contempt prior to investigation." It is taken from a quote that is familiar to recovery programs:

"There is a principle which is a bar against all information, which is proof against all arguments and which cannot fail to keep a man in everlasting ignorance – that principle is *contempt prior to investigation*." Herbert Spencer

Put aside any contempt that you may have about the subject of codependency, and prepare yourself to learn about the variety of ingredients that go into creating this problem, both on the inside and the outside, of you.

The Third Option

INTRODUCTION

Codependency. What is it?
Where did it come from?

T he subject of codependency has been covered extensively in the field of addiction recovery and treatment, primarily as it relates to those who have a relationship with an addict or alcoholic. It was identified as a concept with the founding of Al-Anon in 1951, as spouses of alcoholics began to seek the same benefits their partners were experiencing in recovery. In the 1980's it was thrust into mainstream America with the release of several key books, including Adult Children of Alcoholics in 1983 (Janet G. Woititz), and Codependent No More in 1986 (Melody Beattie). Some say these events are where the subject of codependency really started, but that is far from the truth.

Anything common to mankind will be covered in the Bible. Finding where it is covered can be the challenge, especially where contempt exists for anything that is perceived as new. But Ecclesiastes 1:9 states: *"What has been will be again, what has been done will be done again; there is nothing new under the sun."* Even though the Bible does not use the word specifically, the subject of codependency is covered in the Bible from front to back.

In the 1950's, God simply answered the prayers of suffering people by providing a solution that worked, one that eventually was given a name that had not been used before — codependency. It is not our place to question God's timing, only to accept what He offers and be grateful for the solution. The Hebrews were enslaved in Egypt for over 400 years, and mankind waited thousands of years for Jesus the Messiah to come. God's timing is always right, no matter how long it takes.

What is it? In order to understand the subject of codependency, we must first understand our own personal dependency. As human beings, we are remarkably dependent on other people and the world around us. We were created by God primarily to have a relationship with him and to have relationships with each other. *"So God created human beings in his own image. In the image of God he created them; male and female he created them."* Genesis 1:17. From the first chapter in the Bible we understand that we are an incredible reflection of God himself, not for the purpose of being isolated, but for the purpose of relationship. Healthy relationships are rich in dependency, the kind God intended for us to have. When Jesus stated what the most important aspect of life is, he said, *"Love the Lord your God with all your heart and with all your soul and with all your strength and with all your mind; and, Love your neighbor as yourself."* Luke 10:27. We were created for loving dependent relationships.

"Dependency implies a balance that works," such as the picture of justice being represented by a set of scales in balance. It depends on each side holding its own weight, carrying its own load. One side can exceed the other to a degree and still be in balance, but when one is lighter or heavier than the other, the scales become out of balance and unable to function properly. *"Codependency occurs anytime dependence exceeds the limits that God has established."* When this happens in relationships they become out of balance, and unless corrected will become extreme and dysfunctional. At certain times we do need to "go the extra mile" and "carry each other's burdens," but even those situations demand proper balance to avoid codependency.

The analogy of scales also applies to dependence upon principles or institutions which have good purpose but can become out of balance and dysfunctional, such as our family of origin, churches, and Christian doctrines. It applies as well to our dependence on the world around us, governments, and other the non-human parts of creation. We can just as easily become codependent with creation as we can with humans. This book will expose the vast amount of codependency that exists in our world, which goes way beyond having a relationship with an addict.

Where did it come from? Codependency came when sin entered into the relationship that Adam and Eve had with their Creator. Instead of remaining dependent on God, they decided to create their own rules. Yes, they were influenced by Satan to change the rules in the garden, just as he tried to change the rules in heaven, but it was Adam and Eve who rejected what God said and accepted what Satan offered. *"That is where codependency started, when dependency was set aside for something that looked desirable, believing there was something to gain."* It was their chance to be in control, to have knowledge and decide for themselves what was right and wrong, and they chose this lie over God's truth.

This principle and pattern established in the story of creation, continues to this day. We have a new name for it, but it is the same old trick with the same old results. When dependency becomes codependency, separation occurs that results in consequences, pain, and suffering. There is nothing new under the sun. People still trade the truth for a lie, believing they can be in control and determine right from wrong, but instead of gaining something they experience loss.

Just as addiction is covered in Romans Chapter 1, so are the same basic elements of codependency. At the core of this subject is confusion, about who and what we should be dependent on, and who is ultimately in control. Codependents try to assume control over people and situations they have no control over, — in other words, they play God. *"They exchanged the truth about God for a lie, and worshipped and served created things rather than the Creator—who is forever praised. Amen."* Romans 1:25. Human efforts to play God cause problems. For codependents, it means problems that can be harmful in other people's lives and destructive in their own.

There are a couple of principles to establish that will define much of this book. They were also established in the Garden of Eden and tie directly to the subject of codependency. The first is *"Role Reversal,"* the process by which *"Satan takes what is good and makes it look bad and takes what is bad and makes it look good."* It is amazing how this simple, predictable, and repeatable pattern continues to deceive so many people. Look around the world today for examples where human beings are changing God's rules as set forth in the Bible, taking what is wrong and trying to make it right, and taking what is right and trying to make it wrong. The good is bad and the bad is good. Personal dependency upon God is right and good, but Satan has convinced millions that it is wrong and bad. At the same time what God has established as wrong and bad is being accepted as right and good, especially in the area of sensuality and greed. Dependence on Godly limits has been tossed aside in an effort to gain something, and the result is codependency. This principle was covered by the Prophet Isaiah who wrote: *"Woe to those who call evil good and good evil."* Isaiah 5:20.

While the principle of role reversal has a very broad application, it specifically applies to the subjects of codependency and addiction. God's design for the family is good, with proper balances of love and dependency. The introduction of an addiction into a family creates challenges, ones that most people are actually determined to face. There are instances when people just walk out of the family, but more often than not the family remains engaged in the struggle. However, codependency will cause family members to see recovery principles as confusing and therefore bad, when in fact they are right and good. Instead, families will reverse the role and try to control the addict through various means, such as begging, pleading, manipulating, arguing, pity, shame, guilt, and a host of others. Most likely these methods were learned while growing up from the family of origin, or developed as an adult through life's circumstances. Somehow dependence on God's truth is set aside for what is familiar, making what is bad look good, or at least influences the family to make bad choices.

A common example is when the addict tells stories that are just unbelievable, but the family accepts lies as truth in the name of love. People violate their own conscience, and good people make bad decisions. It is not God's plan. It is role reversal, and the results are bad for everyone. Familiar and comfortable are not always good. Pain has purpose. God never established what was right and good only to change it later and cause confusion. He is the same *"yesterday, today, and forever."* Hebrews 13:8. Our Creator is not the author of this method, but the one who himself tried to reverse roles with God, *"that ancient serpent called the devil, or Satan, who leads the whole world astray."* Revelation 12:9.

The other principle that ties closely to role reversal is *"All-or-Nothing Extremes."* In the garden there were more than two choices, there were many. It was only when sin entered that many of the choices were removed which resulted in consequences, pain, and suffering. There is one subject that is not multiple choice - the subject of salvation through Jesus Christ. There are only two choices, accept or reject. For everything else we are not limited unless codependency is involved. Then it becomes all or nothing, one extreme to the other, over and over and over. This principle seems to have unlimited applications as well, and will be covered throughout this book. But what we need to understand right up front is that the goal is to identify *"The Third Option."*

Through my work in recovery I have been asked countless times to meet with parents of an adult child who has an addiction. They are typically frustrated over their child's addiction and do not know what to do. Many have already received advice from well-meaning family and friends, advice they are not willing to follow. It's just three words — "Kick them out." The implication is that the adult child addict is living at the parent's home, will not get clean and sober, and is creating chaos in the house. People typically do not call for help until the situation is totally out of control. Many times I have talked with one or both of the frustrated parents and basically heard the same thing: "Everyone tells me to kick them out but I do not want to." My response is: "Alright, you don't want to kick them out but you cannot continue the way things are. Let's take those two choices off the table. What is the third option?"

At that point we have a moment of silence, because the parents have no idea what the third option is. They have been stuck in the all-or-nothing extremes of either kicking them out or continuing to put up with their addictive behavior. The third option represents a decision that is a balance between the extremes. Codependency exists in the extremes, and dependency exists in the balance. One is limited to two options; the other starts at the third option and continues to open up possibilities.

Whether or not the addict should stay in the home or be removed is not the point. Each situation is different. But when the only two options are both unacceptable, the family will remain in a dysfunctional state and everyone suffers. The third option is another principle that goes far beyond addiction and codependency. It can be used anytime that opposite extremes are creating only two options, whether personal growth, emotional healing, or spiritual development. For the purpose of codependency it represents freedom for those who feel trapped in someone else's problems or other circumstances of life.

Put the two principles of role reversal and all-or-nothing extremes together and you can see how Satan causes so much confusion with such a simple method. If he can reverse the roles God intended by making what is good look bad or what is bad look good, and remove the choices down to two extremes that are both bad, then he has succeeded in replacing Godly dependency with codependency, and nothing good can come from it. That is why parents, family, and friends of addicts feel so frustrated and hope-less. These situations are made worse when the family tries to make decisions without asking for help from someone who understands the problem, by continuing to try and fix the problem himself or herself. Some of these situations become pure insanity when good people do things their conscience is telling them is wrong but they do it anyway. In the name of love they make decisions that do not make sense, and the love that is good becomes dysfunctional and bad. Everything becomes reversed and extreme as compared to what God intends.

If this is true, is it then possible for a Christian to be a codependent? The answer is not only yes, but many Christians are codependent and do not even know it. They have no idea what it is or where it came from. It is like having mustard on your face; other people can see it but you can't. God help the person who points it out. Rarely do codependents appreciate the truth, because for them dysfunction has become the norm, especially in the area of personal relationships. Common responses from codependents are to attack the messenger or run and hide. It usually takes a crisis to break down the barrier called denial and accept the truth. Often that crisis comes in the form of someone's addiction. That is how role reversal and all-or-nothing extremes will take even a Christian to the land of illusion, where the truth is bad and the choices are few. Knowing God and the Bible does not prevent codependency. The truth is these can actually foster codependency when a lack of wisdom or denial is present.

There is a question that I have developed to help people see how this is possible. It works when talking with a person who has identified himself or herself as a Christian, who is trying to help someone else with an addiction, but cannot see how they are actually enabling the addict's behavior. The question is this: "*Can you violate a scriptural principle from the Bible and get a blessing from God?*" The only honest answer is "no." Then I talk about Galatians 6:7 which states, "*Do not be deceived: God cannot be mocked. A man reaps what he sows.*" What I try to help people understand is that praying for God to help the addict, then interrupting the process of reaping and sowing by rescuing the addict, will only nullify their prayers. God would have to bless the violation of a principle that He established, which is not going to happen. Codependency causes people who know God and the Bible to actually violate the very principles they believe in. Christian codependents are living in a reversed role from what God intends, and are typically focused on external circumstances.

"*Codependents are externally-focused people in a constantly changing world.*" For example, if the children are good you are a good parent, but if they are bad you are a bad parent. Neither of these is true, but for the codependent they are the only two choices. It is all based on external conditions that are beyond the codependent's control, but role reversal makes it impossible to see. God's definition of what a good parent is has been replaced with bad emotions. Shame and guilt become the motivators, manipulation and control the tools. The all-or-nothing extremes are expressed by the codependent in passive/aggressive behavior that only makes things worse. A dysfunctional attempt to control the situation results in more pain, because "*external validation never heals internal wounds.*" It is a vicious cycle that is void of Godly dependence and saturated in codependency. Without recovery or treatment there is little hope. It's just too overwhelming to solve alone. I'll share an example of a good role in life being turned into something bad through codependency.

Ruth E. #3 is a codependent that sought recovery through our ministry. Her brother was an addict who had been rescued continually over a period of five years by Ruth E. #3 and her mother. Through support groups and reading they began to understand the elements of codependency and how they both had been violating the Biblical principles of reaping and sowing. Progress was made and when the enabling stopped, her brother suddenly decided that treatment was a good idea. Five years of prayers and frustration with no results, and just a few months into genuine recovery good things were starting to happen.

Then, out of the blue, Ruth E. #3 called in a panic. Her brother had notified her mom that his life was in danger at the treatment center. It seems there was major drug trafficking going on there and the staff was in on it. Mom and sis were ready to jump in the car and go save him, but paused long enough to make a call. We talked about removing the two options of rescuing and doing nothing, and if there was a third option. Old habits were resurfacing, making it difficult to see what other options were available, but she had already embraced change and was calling to ask for help. I suggested that a call to the program director was in order, and if that if they still were not satisfied then call the local police who could properly handle this dangerous situation. Of course, the brother's plot to escape was foiled with a call to the director, and more importantly two people's lives were not controlled by the lies of an addict.

This example demonstrates that if the violations of Scripture are removed then good decisions can begin to be made. This is not an overnight experience, it is a process called recovery that will produce results. It relates as well to an Old Testament scripture that has been around for thousands of years. "*A hot-tempered person must pay the penalty; rescue them, and you will have to do it again.*" Proverbs 19:19. Do not get distracted by the example of "a hot-tempered person" and miss the warning of repeated rescuing. God has established a principle that will not change; rescuing someone from the consequences of their actions will lead to doing it again. Correcting the violation and returning to what is right and good is the correct choice, and represents the third option.

It is important to understand that many of the personal examples of codependency have nothing to do with addiction. There are people who are stuck in pre-determined roles in life and for some reason they cannot break free. Often these are based on the expectations of the family or parents, even if the person affected is now an adult. Others go from one bad relationship to another, never seeing that their own misguided dependence is the cause. Then we have examples of people who mask their emotional and spiritual problems with performance-based identities, such as successful business people, athletes, and those in leadership roles. Their codependency is really about people pleasing and acceptance. Still others lead compassionate lives of service, as missionaries or caregivers or something similar, but no matter where they go codependency surfaces and causes trouble.

The analogy of codependents being like "salsa" helps to understand the varying degrees of codependency, and how to interact with people who have this problem. If you don't have any experience with salsa, you might not know the difference between hot and mild unless someone tells you. Codependents can be found everywhere in varying degrees, but they all have the same basic ingredients. If you're not familiar with the problem of codependency you might think you are dealing with a mild one, only to find out by experience they are actually flaming hot. It can help if someone familiar with the problems tells you what they are but most of the time, you just have to experience it for yourself. Even with people who have been identified as codependents, meaning others are aware of their "label," you still have to learn how to read the label and interpret the ingredients. Are they mild? Are they flaming? It gets tricky when you find a good codependent who tries to hide their label, often putting something over the top that is false information about what is really inside, a deception to hide the ingredients. An experienced person can call it for what it is; someone else might not be as perceptive as wind up getting burned by surprise.

"The truth is that all human beings are codependent to some degree." The individual part comes in understanding the degrees of codependency and numerous ways that it can be expressed. While some people are flaming codependents because of the damage and

harm caused to others, there are others who have a much milder version that is still not healthy but not nearly as destructive. They are good people who make the best decisions they can, but usually have some issues that are affecting the quality of their decisions. Most people are somewhere between the flaming and the mild in varying degrees. Their symptoms may be common but the way they are expressed is different. All can benefit from healing and recovery. One of the main purposes of this book is help people identify their level of codependency, determine where it is coming from, and know how to recover from it. This may require an honest look at issues that have been avoided or suppressed. Readers should keep in mind that exposing an issue does not create the problem; it just brings it into the light where it can be solved. It takes deliberate action to transform codependency into healthy dependence.

Since codependency is such a diversified problem, having a one-word description is really inadequate. Underneath the umbrella of the word is a host of human expressions, identified primarily by people's actions and words. The way people interact at home, work, and in public are often the most revealing factors. It comes out at school functions, meetings, and public gatherings. It could be said that where two or more are gathered someone is a codependent. If people are going to make the connection between themselves and the subject of codependency, then more descriptions are needed that are simple and will connect the person to the problem. This book will provide quite a few descriptions that are meant to help identify the problem without replacing the word codependency. The word is accurate, the degrees are diverse. Chapter Two will provide titles and analogies of flaming and mild codependents.

There are so many factors that contribute to how each person is affected that it is also impossible for all examples to fit every person. And since denial of truth is a key element of codependency, people will look for reasons to pronounce themselves an exception. They will pick out a single example, establish that it does not describe them, and then dismiss the whole possibility of being codependent. Nothing in this book will have an impact if the purpose of reading it is to find exceptions, try to figure out how someone else is a codependent, or find a new method of fixing other people.

The real purpose of this book is to identify obstacles and provide solutions. The path to solutions is a journey inward, not outward. "*The hardest truth for a codependent to accept is that in order to change the circumstances they have to change themselves.*" Resistance of this truth is futile; the real life testimonies prove otherwise. If codependency at its core is a disruption in our dependence on God, then re-establishing that dependence internally is the answer. The obstacles can be huge and it might be painful to face them but one thing is for sure, they are all on the inside even if they were caused by external circumstances. So one goal of this book is to identify personal codependency traits and remove the internal obstacles that are preventing spiritual, emotional, and mental freedom. This is not a book about boundaries; the award-winning materials by Dr. John Townsend and Dr. Henry Cloud will help you with those. Nor is it intended to replace any of the valuable resources that already exist, just add to the overall effort to help suffering people identify their codependent problems and provide solutions.

In recovery, codependency is an evasive issue proven by the fact that the point of relapse is almost impossible to determine. For example, when an addict relapses they get drunk or high. But what about a codependent? Where is the point of relapse? It may be that each codependent has to define it for themselves, with a lot of honesty and help from others. Keep in mind that if addiction recovery is present, the addict's sobriety date is not the codependent's also, and if the addict relapses it does not mean the codependent relapsed as well. The idea that everything depends on the addict getting clean and sober is a delusional mindset. That would mean the good life is dependent on someone not getting high or drunk, and that is not a good life. What happens when they drink or use drugs? It means everyone else's peace in life just went away because of the actions of one person. Pure codependency. Each person establishes their own recovery and determines when it started, and when it resets.

It is important also to note that codependents can either be male or female. It seems to affect more women than men, but there is good cause to believe it is more equal than what is openly admitted. Men seem to either fly under the radar by hiding their emotions, or they are aggressive codependents that succeed in the professional arena so it makes them look good. In either case male codependents typically do not do well in close personal relationships, most often revealed in how they handle conflict or engage in rescuing others. Throughout the book this element of codependency will be covered in more detail. For now it is a point of acceptance that the problem is not gender-specific.

Ron E. #1 is the father of an adult addict. He called me one night to discuss the struggles he was having with his son. It was one of the most unique situations I have come across. He described how he had been giving his son $30 a day for 20 years. That was my moment of silence, not sure I had heard him correctly. Then the obvious question about little junior's age — he was 38 years old. More questions clarified that the son didn't work, was receiving his allowance each day in cash, and that Ron E. #1 was providing a home for him as well on the same property but in a separate building. Resisting the urge to ask if I could get the same deal, we persevered to the reason he called which was to ask for help. After some discussion he made the statement that "if my son would just quit drinking I would not be an enabler." I told him that I had bad news — if his son quit drinking he would still be an enabler. At that point he said that his wife had been telling him the same thing. I suggested he listen.

Not much was really accomplished on that call. I hadn't heard from him before and haven't since, but it makes one point perfectly clear: codependency is not gender-specific. It also demonstrates how people can believe that internal growth is dependent on external circumstances, and that the answer is for someone else to change first. This is never true, unless codependency has led to role reversal where everything depends on someone else and not on God.

Another aspect of codependency is the way it plays out culturally. Not only does it reach beyond gender and addictions but it also reaches through media, speaking more on a national and international level. The media is dependent upon the negative circumstances of the world for news with a token of positive reporting, but are generally codependent with the way they handle the news and what they use it for. Codependency can often be expressed by taking a small amount of truth, combining it with a lot of fantasy or lies, and then calling it real truth. The media is the same, since they are only responsible for some version of the truth while representing it as complete truth, hand-picking those parts, which will draw emotion. Externally-focused in a constantly changing world, reversing the roles of what is good and bad, reporting in all-or-nothing extremes. It is surprising how people are deceived into believing that what they see on the news is actually truth. Manipulation and control of public opinion is more of the goal. Dependence on the media for truth is really codependency from both sides. That's just one example of how the world around us is full of codependency.

This book is intended for:
- The codependent that is out of control and causing harm to others.
- Those who are mildly codependent but want to be free from its influence.
- Adults who grew up with codependent parents.
- Christians who cannot understand why they never have peace and joy in their lives, and cannot seem to get along with other people, especially at church.

- The woman who has identified codependency as her problem but has been told it is not real and is just a subject for talk shows.
- Anyone in a leadership role in a church.
- People who have the spiritual gifts of compassion and mercy.
- Addicts who are clean and sober but unable to explain why their primary recovery is not resolving their deeper problems in relationships.
- Those who are not addicts but know they have the same addictive tendencies.
- The parent who lost a son or daughter to addiction, and lives with the guilt of believing it was their fault or that they could have prevented it.
- Families of addicts who are frustrated and out of options.
- The man who thinks aggressive domination is an asset, but has persistent conflict with other people and institutions.
- The man who thinks rescuing women is admirable.
- Those who want to change but feel obligated to pre-determined roles and do not know how to break free.
- Anyone who cannot explain to another person what codependency is.

If this book is successful it will hurt. Hitting the nerve of codependency causes pain; there is no way around it. I have taught on this subject for many years, and it has been part of my own personal recovery. Being able to effectively teach about codependency without seeing pain in the eyes of the audience would be nice, but it rarely happens.

The use of an analogy has worked well to prepare the audience for the subject. It involves standing in front of the group and declaring boldly that they are all Eskimos (if you happen to be an Eskimo just use Blonde Surfer). Then I persist by stating that I am going to prove they are all Eskimos and there is no use trying to deny it. This brief attempt is followed by pointing out that no one was affected by my comments, but if I had said, "you are an enabler," a different response would take place inside the person, one that might be uncomfortable or even painful. The analogy concludes by pointing out there is no difference on my end from the two statements. The difference takes place in the heart of the individual.

Simply put, this book cannot create pain inside of you. It can only connect with something that is already there and expose it. When that happens, just realize it represents a key area for growth. Make a note and keep going. The only way to fail is to quit. Are you ready to begin?

1

All Addicts are Codependents

A professional counselor once said that the hardest thing to get people to understand is when there is an addict in the family it is an "addicted" family.

This concept was illustrated during a PBS special in the 1980's where John Bradshaw taught from his book "Healing the Shame That Binds You." By using a hanging mobile with several components, he explained that when one part of the mobile moves, all the other parts move as well. This was applied to the idea that when one person in the family is addicted, all other parts of the family are affected. This does not change with the type of chemical, drug, or booze that is used; it remains common through all addictions. Family members are quick to dismiss this type of label if they can find exceptions between themselves and those "other people," but that is just denial and dishonesty.

Codependents prefer to think that they are nothing like the addict, but if that is true then how come so much of the codependent's character comes out when dealing with an addict? The dividing line between addicts and codependents is often self-imposed just to create a difference, whether it exists or not. If one goes to a recovery meeting for codependents he/she will encounter some degree of the "us vs. them" mentality. It is certainly nothing unique to codependency; it is pretty common to human nature in general. So is the difference between addicts and codependents that significant? Not really. After all, we do call addiction "chemical dependency."

Addicts are actually dependent to an extreme. They depend on the drug or booze to produce a high. As the cycle continues they become dependent on others to take care of them or make excuses for their lifestyle, and eventually they become dependent on the codependent. The length of time this process takes is not critical, but the dynamic of unhealthy dependence is. Just below the surface of addiction is codependency, where the addict is being dependent on something external to fix a problem that is internal.

The challenge for an addict in the early stages of recovery is to stay clean and sober. Whether a person is delivered instantly or through a process does not remove the need for a personal housecleaning and the making of amends for wrongs done. Either way it is not an overnight event, and typically takes a few years to truly make amends and learn to face life's challenges without getting drunk or high. A period of genuine recovery will then cause codependent issues to surface.

"Somewhere between three and five years into the recovery process, addicts should come face to face with their own codependency." It sits beneath the layers of addictive behaviors, or to use a recovery term their "character defects." Some people use the analogy of an onion to illustrate this principle, describing how peeling off the layers reveals more of what is underneath. A common phrase that is used to describe this process is "more will be revealed." For the person who continues to grow in recovery, the primary program for addiction will not work on the secondary issue of codependency. That would violate the most fundamental principle of recovery. Where an alcoholic can help another alcoholic when no one else can, an addict can do the same for another addict, and a codependent for another codependent. This is not

a mix-and-match principle; there are separate recovery meetings for each problem for a reason.

In my personal recovery I was three years clean and sober when I hit this roadblock. I went to my sponsor for help and he told me he had no idea what I was dealing with, but his wife recognized it as codependency. She served as the literature person for her recovery group and provided a pamphlet for him to pass along: "Boundaries for Codependents" by Rokelle Lerner (Hazelden Publishing). It was like reading my autobiography. It described the emotional, mental, spiritual, and physical aspects of codependency. I had them all. The timing was also driven by circumstances in life, and my inability to resolve character issues through my primary recovery. I worked hard at my recovery, but nothing was working on the current issues. I was simply in the wrong program to deal with codependency.

There was an event that took place, which was the last straw for me, one that was so embarrassing and frustrating that I had to find an answer. The episode that I brought to my sponsor took place over 25 years ago, yet even today I would prefer to put some generic name on it and pretend like it wasn't me. Codependency causes people to do things that are embarrassing to admit, shameful and full of negative emotions, but honesty aides the healing process. Such was the case with this event.

The marriage to my children's mother was still together when I got clean and sober, but at three years into my recovery and Christian life, we were living in two different worlds and our union was coming apart. We were separated, and since we had three children I moved out and was staying with my parents. She and the three boys stayed in the house where we had all lived together. I still went over there to see the children and at some level kept hope that the marriage would survive. Those who understand codependency will see the red flags in this story already, but at that time I could not.

One night I went there to visit, and as I was walking out the door to leave an argument occurred. When I got to the car I was upset at myself for arguing. After all I was a Christian now and clean and sober, so I should have been better than that. I would later learn more about my own expectations, false guilt, and perfectionism. I decided to be a really good guy and went back up to the door to apologize, but before I could get off the porch and back to the car, another argument. There I was, back in car, upset again, heaping loads of condemnation on myself. So I went back to the door to apologize with a firm commitment that I would not, under any circumstances, for any reason, argue. It did not work. One more trip to the car with more regrets. The truly embarrassing part is that I actually did this five times before finally leaving that night, and was wiped out mentally and emotionally.

That is what I asked my sponsor for help with, and he was completely confused. He had no idea why I would do something like that. But the pamphlet was not confusing, and as I read through the words it described all the mental, emotional, spiritual, and even physical aspects of that night. There was a word for the condition I was dealing with, codependency, and it was being revealed through a total lack of boundaries. I began to understand the problem, and trusted the guidance of the pamphlet for the solution.

I also began going once each week to a recovery meeting for people who were codependents like me. I had already learned from my primary recovery that if you want results you have to follow directions and do the work. The principles for this issue were not too complicated; applying them was a whole different story. Slowly, one step at a time, I began to see changes in how I responded to people and situations. More was revealed as I began to see these traits were evident in almost every area of my life, especially at work. One significant moment of clarity came when I got an honest look at the true condition of my codependency, and wondered how in the world I had stayed sober with all this "junk" inside of me. How could I have not seen any of it? It was extremely discouraging and difficult to accept. I had questions and doubts about the value of my primary recovery and my relationship with God. It is not a warm and fuzzy experience to see the true condition of codependency in your own life.

I also learned another important principle: *"things get worse before they get better."* Seeing the truth did not change anything, it only made change possible. Taking the action was uncomfortable and painful for a while, but I was told that as long as I did not quit it would get better. Looking ahead made the challenge seem endless, but with a genuine effort it took only a short period of time to experience positive changes. It proved there were times when I could not trust my own feelings and thoughts and had to trust God and other people, and follow directions. Codependents like to give directions, but they don't like to follow them.

The answer to my hidden problem was the analogy of the onion. I was not ready to see it until a period of primary recovery was achieved, enough to remove shortcomings and expose the other issues. I have since worked with many others who find they have codependent issues which surface between three to five years of their primary recovery. When something is hidden in the dark, shining the light of truth does not create what was hidden, it only reveals it. Some people are ready to see what is hidden, and others are not.

There are also people I have met who have more than five years of recovery and refuse to accept, acknowledge, or work on these codependent issues when they arise. They become dysfunctional and sober, and, from what I have witnessed, arrive at one of three outcomes; they either relapse or quit recovery, get help for the secondary issue, or manage to stay clean and sober and just become repetitive in meetings. They are the people with long-term sobriety that are complacent and stagnant in their growth, who say the same things over and over and over, year after year after year. Why anyone would be satisfied to remain in that condition for years and decades is beyond me, but it happens.

It also happens to people in other organizations, such as church. People who surrender their lives to God and live an abundant life for a while, then somewhere about three to five years later discover character problems. They will quit going to church, get help for their problems, or manage to stay in church and become Sunday morning pew warmers. They are the people with long term church membership that are stagnant in their growth and complacent, who become repetitive in their religious duties. *"Codependency comes in many forms and is not just a problem that surfaces when dealing with an addict."*

So not too long after this personal moment of clarity, when I was beginning to see some results from codependent recovery, scene two of the driveway movie took place. There I was, at the house where my family was living, in the car in the driveway, having determined with all sincerity to leave without arguing, but failed yet another mission. And that is where the similarities end. I sat there for a minute, with all the old "junk" coming up telling me that I was a bad person if I did not go and apologize. This time though I used a few simple tools of recovery, put the car in reverse, and drove away. I was not wiped out, did not feel horrible. I had peace. Yes, I had failed to not argue, and made mistakes in the process, but I had learned the tools of codependent recovery and, thank God, they worked. As I drove away there was nothing but gratitude to God and the recovery program.

And while the growth that started at that time in my life has been gradual and continues to this day, that night was the turning point. Avoidance never changed anything for me; it came through pain, honesty, and a desire to face my problems. I consider that my point of achieving "sobriety" for codependency, emotional, mental, spiritual, and indeed physical. I never want to be that person again.

The reason I believe some people choose not to accept that they are a codependent as well as an addict is because they have just enough peace and comfort to get by on. Perhaps the emotional pain is too much to face, or their life growing up was abusive and they are determined to forget their past. Whatever the cause, there is one factor these people will never get around: *"success in primary recovery does not produce success with secondary issues."* I met one man who made it over 15 years in his primary recovery before facing his codependent issues, which became extreme over that period of time. It was amazing to see the transformation, but by his own admission he could only wish that he had not waited so long.

How does this subject then apply the other way around, directly to the theme of this book? If we look at the title of this chapter in a slightly different way, we can say that *"all addicts are codependents in the sense that all codependents are really addicts."* The codependent is addicted to control, lies, fantasies, and delusion, and quite often they are addicted to the addict. Flaming codependents have toxic relationships built on dysfunctional extremes, where the only goal is blame the other person for the problems. Relationships for mild codependents are emotionally unhealthy and may not be as intoxicating, but they do alter the state of the person enough to achieve denial, avoidance, or false guilt. Some codependents are addicted to anything outside of themselves. Other codependents are simply addicted to negative emotions, ones that produce internal chemicals in the brain the same as lust works for a sex addict. These chemicals are also released with rage, pride, self-righteous criticism, or extreme emotional reactions. A codependent will say with authority, "I don't need this," when the truth is they really do need the stress, anger, and chaos to avoid looking at themselves. Their drug of choice comes in many forms, the same as the drug addict or alcoholic.

The reality of my own experience working with families when an active addict involved supports the comment at the beginning of the chapter from the counselor. The hardest thing to do is get the family to accept that the addict is not the source of all the problems; they are just the most obvious excuse. It seems that the common belief is that if the addict will stop using and stay clean and sober, then everything will be just fine. They would assume from the illustration of the hanging mobile that one part can swing out of control without affecting or moving any other parts, which is impossible. It is either an accurate analogy or it is a total lie. Perhaps Bradshaw chose that example because the hardest thing for him to do was getting people to accept the truth. That is how the codependent is addicted to the addict. It gives them a reason to avoid themselves, a little at first, then with increased dependency, and eventually they are hooked on being externally focused in a constantly changing world. The farther a person goes down this path of codependency, the more dysfunctional they will become, emotionally, mentally, and spiritually. Their physical health will decline as well as they progress from mild to flaming.

Looking closer at the idea that codependency is not just about a relationship with an addict, we can further understand this subject by looking at an underlying human condition, "validation." God created us with the need to be validated by Him and other people. Dr. James Dobson has spoken to the idea that what we think about ourselves will be greatly affected by what we think the most important person in our lives thinks about us. Some people will try to push back on this idea by claiming they do not care what other people think, which is just an effort to somehow prove they are impenetrable. But if that is truly the goal, then they can have it. *"Loving dependent relationships are built on giving and receiving validation from the right sources according to God's standards."*

Validation means "recognition or affirmation that a person or their feelings or opinions are valid or worthwhile." Children need to be validated to know they are loved, which might explain why some adults struggle with this issue. Important phases of emotional, mental, and spiritual development that are missed will not just vanish with time. An adult with unmet needs will find a way to meet those needs, mostly in dysfunctional ways. This is one reason God has described himself as our Heavenly Father, the one who can bring validation into our lives no matter what our experiences have been. When we open our hearts to Christ we are validated as

God's children, then the Holy Spirit lives in us as an authentic seal of ownership. It is the highest level of validation we can receive from God, to be called children of the Most High. *"And you also were included in Christ when you heard the word of truth, the gospel of your salvation. Having believed, you were marked in him with a seal, the promised Holy Spirit."* Ephesians 1:13.

Another way God provides validation is through His Word, the Bible. It provides instructions on how to live and conduct ourselves in this world. As such, it also provides limits or boundaries that keep our lives in balance and out of extremes. It establishes what is good and what is bad, never reversing roles later to cause confusion. We have a choice to accept or reject the Bible as God's "feelings or opinions (that) are valid and worthwhile." Accepting these limits is how we demonstrate that God is the most important influence in our lives. The affirmation and recognition we receive for choosing to live by His rules are called blessings. However, if we choose to reverse the roles and live by our own rules that violate the Bible, then we get consequences. If we choose instead to live by God's standards then we are validated through loving dependent relationships with God and other people. Applying the analogy of the scales from the Introduction, we can show there is a balance between the validation we receive emotionally, mentally, spiritually, and physically. When received from the proper source it will lead to healthy dependence, if not it will become codependency.

For example, we need God's love that is unconditional, while at the same time we need human love and affection. For the deeper and more personal levels of physical intimacy, God established the marriage relationship. When people give and receive this type of validation within the marriage relationship, then a loving dependent relationship will develop. It still requires other factors to form healthy intimacy, but when people try to get their sexual validation outside of marriage, the only possible outcome is consequences. It doesn't happen immediately, just a little at first. But eventually they are hooked on unhealthy dependent relationships.

If God establishes a standard then it is right, no matter how many people disagree. These people are externally validated, reversing the roles of good and bad, living in extremes that are out of balance. Always searching, never satisfied, developing increased dependency over time and arriving at codependency. There is an old song performed by Johnny Lee that states this condition the best, "Looking for Love in All the Wrong Places."

It helps to sort out the concept of validation by comparing it to distinct and separate "cards," such as the type that are used for access to controlled areas. At the manufacturing plant where I formerly worked, there was a guarded security gate at the entrance, as well as electronic door locks inside the plant. Anyone entering the plant had to show the proper identification badge to pass through the security gate. Otherwise the security guard would stop that person and grant access under different rules, or not at all. Once in the plant, some areas were open for general access and others were controlled with electronic keypads that were activated by an additional card. The card did not have to touch the device; it could be validated by coming in close proximity to the sensors in the device. I had two cards on my lanyard at all times that worked for entrance into general and controlled areas. Using the proper card at the proper time was necessary to use the system as it was programmed to work. It would validate my identity based on the way it had been set up ahead of time by the programmer. I could choose how to use my cards, but they only worked properly when used according the way it was designed.

In personal relationships we have the same type of conditions that were created by God. Access into our lives should have limits and boundaries that are defined, which are based on truth and knowledge from God. We should not just open our personal lives to all people, as some are not safe. We can be open to people in general by granting access as acquaintances or friends. Only those people who have special permission should be allowed into our lives at an intimate level. This represents good boundaries that define healthy dependence in relationships. When these guidelines are not followed — when what is good becomes bad and what is bad becomes good — then the roles are reversed and dysfunctional relationships will result. Adults who were abused as children will struggle with these concepts, because their sense of trust and limits were damaged. This explains why victims of abuse get into abusive relationships as adults. They let unsafe people into their lives at an intimate level. Children raised in a codependent family will do the same; for all the wrong reasons, they will give access into their own lives or try to gain access into the lives of others.

As we look at this principle further, keep in mind that the Creator of this world designed the system that it operates under. He made the rules. He established what is right and wrong. When someone breaks a rule it does not make the rule wrong, it makes the person wrong. Laws do not force people to obey them; there is still a personal choice that results in consequences when the law is violated. People can steal and not get caught, but that does not make them any less of a thief. Their consequences might just be delayed or avoided. So it is with the boundaries that God established. His laws do not force people to obey them. It is still a choice. People can get away with violating His laws for a time but they are not innocent. Their consequences might come later, but unlike a human system that can be avoided, a violation of God's laws will always have consequences. It can be delayed but never avoided, unless there is divine intervention.

Taking these principles about our need for validation, how God created us, and the analogy of having certain cards, we can understand that we are created with basically four types of "Validation Cards." When used properly, within the limits that God has established, we can have healthy relationships because we are following the system as it was programmed by the designer. When people try to create their own way of getting validated, they will have to violate the rules to get what they want, how and when they want it. In other words, they use a functional system in a dysfunctional manner.

The first set of validation cards represents a set of four "Healthy Cards." This is what God created us with for the purpose of receiving validation. They were designed individually with a purpose for either general or controlled areas of our lives. Using the proper card at the proper time is critical to have loving, dependent relationships. The system was programmed long before any of us were born, so we are just responsible for the way we use it. Attempting to change the system or compromise its integrity will only lead to trouble.

The first healthy validation card is the "Acquaintance Card," which represents living in the world with other people, ones that we meet in public or through being in the same place at the same time. These are people that we do not already know or people we know casually. They can be people we meet waiting in line at a store or sit next to on an airplane. It can also represent people we work with or those who belong to the same organization, such as church or recovery groups, or maybe participating in a sports team for our children or ourselves. We do not know everyone at work or in society on the same level. Some we are just acquainted with, while others are more personal friends. Have you ever met someone who is an acquaintance and before you know it they are telling you personal details about their life? Ones that you really do not want to know? These are people with damaged Acquaintance Cards trying to get validated by anyone who will listen. It is an example of using the wrong card at the wrong time for the wrong reason, which comes from a lack of healthy boundaries, and most likely from someone who has trouble with intimate relationships.

The next healthy validation card is a "Friendship Card," which represents people who have gained more access to our lives than a mere acquaintance. These are people that we know and trust, so access is available at an appropriate level. There are different levels of friendship as well — some are new friends, and others have known us for a long time. Good friends are ones that we can be accountable to, such as a person who can tell us concerns they see in our life. More access into our lives is given to these people because we come to know and trust them, based on knowledge and truth. This is not based on frequency of contact; some of the best friends we can have are those we see infrequently, but they know us well and there is mutual respect. Sometimes we meet people and form a friendship in a short period of time, which is a great experience if it is based on wisdom and truth. The problem comes when people grant this access to the wrong people, such as con artists who gain the trust of people only to steal from them. Afterward these people wonder why they could not see it coming, but fail to recognize they used a Friendship Card with someone who was barely an acquaintance. Deceitful people know they have to gain access into people's lives before they can take anything from them. Recognizing a fake card is possible when one knows what to look for, or have healthy enough cards to recognize a fraudulent one sees it.

A friend was talking about a man he met who was an expert on counterfeit money. Out of curiosity he asked this man how he could know all the different types of fake money, with so many types of currency, and new ways of making counterfeits. The expert replied that he never studied the fake money; he only studied the real currency so that he could easily recognize a counterfeit when he saw it. The best way to protect ourselves against bad people is to be the best we can be personally. Healthy people attract healthy people and will have the ability to help others without being deceived. Practicing good limits and boundaries with the Friendship Card will lead people to saying "yes" and "no" when they should, and being able to hear the same from others.

Understanding the principles of codependency and the use of Acquaintance and Friendship cards is critical to making progress away from unhealthy lifestyles. People with codependency will allow access into their lives from the wrong people and try to gain access into other people's lives when they should not. This can be as simple as giving unwanted advice, such as making suggestive comments designed to help the other person, which is just manipulation. A healthy person will ask someone else if they want help and accept "no" as an answer without becoming a martyr. Proper use of these two cards will lead to better friendships. More complicated examples are when codependents try to rescue other people, either from the consequences of their actions, or from their struggles in their life. Codependent rescuers can be dangerous people who should not be trusted, but improper use of validation cards will provide them access into the lives of others and produce victims.

Codependents are boundary busters, and it does not matter if it is an acquaintance, friend, or intimate relationship; all represent opportunity for influence or control. When a person decides to change, they have to learn to set boundaries for themselves and others, which requires knowing when and where to set them. A common first step for many is to say "no" to people who have been taking advantage of them, even when it is family. They are "people pleasers" who have been getting their validation by trying to make everyone happy, who feel unappreciated and invalidated. To make changes they will have to realize who made the poor choices in the first place.

The third healthy validation card is the "Intimacy Card." This one represents the deepest level of internal access into our lives, and is intended as controlled access for certain people. It grants special access for close relationships, intended as a closed environment that needs to be protected. God designed us with this element, but gave us free will to use it. For marriage the Bible has specific instructions, with limits on how it can be used. We are told that "*the fear of the* LORD *is the beginning of knowledge, but fools despise wisdom and instruction.*" Proverbs 1:7. The fear spoken of here is "respect" of the Lord and his design for living. There are also people who want to live their own way, by their own rules, satisfying their needs their own way. This scripture calls them "foolish," an accurate description considering the damage caused by misuse of this card. It is possible to have intimacy outside of marriage with friends, not physical intimacy of a sexual nature, but emotional and spiritual intimacy that exceed mere friendship. This also needs to be kept in proper context through wisdom and understanding. *"How much better to get wisdom than gold, to get insight rather than silver!"* Proverbs 16:16. This card carries with it the greatest rewards in relationships, and the biggest consequences from violations.

The fourth and last healthy validation card is the "Salvation Card," which is obtained through faith in Jesus Christ only. There is restricted access to a place called Heaven, where all other cards are invalid. When Jesus was talking to a crowd he was asked a question: *"Lord, are only a few people going to be saved?"* He said to them, *"Make every effort to enter through the narrow door, because many, I tell you, will try to enter and will not be able to."* Luke 13:23-24. This card does not come with birth; it is acquired free of charge based on the sacrificial death of Jesus on the cross, and his resurrection from the dead. When we believe in Jesus as our Lord and Savior, then a deposit is put into our hearts that seals our eternal destiny. *"And you also were included in Christ when you heard the message of truth, the gospel of your salvation. When you believed, you were marked in him with a seal, the promised Holy Spirit, who is a deposit guaranteeing our inheritance until the redemption of those who are God's possession — to the praise of his glory."* Ephesians 1:13-14. This and other scriptures make clear one certain thought regarding this card: don't leave earth without it. When people try to create their own Salvation Card by making up ways to get to heaven, it might give them personal validation while on the earth, especially if they can get others to buy into their plan, but it will be revealed as a counterfeit when looked at by the One who created the authentic card.

A few other aspects for all four healthy validation cards: they are not black and white; they each have a unique color and a sense of appeal. There is individual recognition of each one, they are not blurred together, and have distinct characteristics. This means with healthy cards we can be clear about our relationships and the boundaries that exist with each of the four. Acquaintance is different than friendship, which is different than intimacy. In the context of good boundaries, we make decisions based on truth, wisdom, and understanding when a person is allowed a deeper level of access into our lives. Acquaintances are not mixed up with intimate relationships. Salvation through Christ is unique, not to be mixed up with the myriad of other ways into heaven people have created on their own. Healthy cards represent healthy boundaries, ones that need to be respected in order to have loving dependent relationships. Otherwise, it becomes dysfunctional and eventually codependent.

We also need to keep our expectations in check. The only person to ever have a perfect set of cards was Jesus Christ, because he took on human form and lived on earth without sin. *"For we do not have a high priest who is unable to empathize with our weaknesses, but we have one who has been tempted in every way, just as we are — yet he did not sin."* Hebrews 4:15. He was faced with emotional, mental, spiritual, and physical challenges beyond what most of us will ever experience, yet he never sinned and remained the perfect Savior. The original plan for humans in the Garden of Eden was to have all healthy cards and get validation directly from God. Sin changed all that, and now even the best we can do is still stained with it. Repairing damaged cards and cleaning up the stains of sin is a combination of our actions and God's grace (*faith without works is dead.* James 2:26). We have a choice to accept or reject what He offers us, and then the grace that exceeds understanding can work in our lives. *"Now to him who is able to do immeasurably more than all we ask or imagine, according to his power that is at work within us."* Ephesians 3:20. The goal is not perfection, but until we leave this earth there will always be a personal need to clean up internally and repair our validation cards.

One of the clear violations of the Intimacy Card is when people create their own standards by saying if you feel affection towards another person, and then experience the full potential by having sex with them. That is taking a gift God provided for the purpose of intimacy and using it in the wrong way. It is a distortion of truth, and will result in problems. People try to claim these activities are expressions of intimacy, by redefining what the word means to fit their own purpose. They can get away with violating God's law for a time, but they are not innocent. This idea is being promoted for both youth and adults, regardless of age or gender. Instead of respecting boundaries established by God, just get your validation from whatever source makes you feel good. The Bible calls that "lust," and recorded 2,000 years ago that people "*were inflamed with lust for one another.*" Romans 1:27. This is actually a repetitive problem throughout history, because "*what has been will be again, what has been done will be done again; there is nothing new under the sun.*" Ecc. 1:9.

Another example is adult people who take their Intimacy Card and go around waving it in public, getting recognition and smiles from the opposite sex. We call those people "flirts," and some are already married. They are getting validated from the wrong source, depending on an external response to make them feel good inside. They do not have to make physical contact with the other person. They just come into close proximity and wave their card to get validated, but that only fools them into thinking they are not doing anything wrong. God obviously disapproves, but people push aside His standards and create their own rules. Certain people become so called "experts" and get television shows, write books, and become advisors on how relationships should work. One such expert was quoted as saying that it was acceptable for married men to lust after women other than their spouses, as long as they took their lust home and expressed it with their wife.

That's a good example of the foolishness of mankind as compared to the wisdom of the One who created intimacy. *"It is role reversal, taking what is bad and making it look good, creating alternate rules for living outside of God's limits."*

Jesus even clarified this issue when he said, *"You have heard that it was said, 'You shall not commit adultery.' But I tell you that anyone who looks at a woman lustfully has already committed adultery with her in his heart."* Matthew 5:27-28. The limits that God established for marriage did not include getting validated outside of the relationship by lusting. Rejection of this limit has caused immense consequences, pain, and suffering in our world. Codependency is an accurate term for this condition, because the marriage should be internally focused for validation with limits and boundaries. Instead, it becomes externally focused in a constantly changing world, reversing the roles of good and bad, living in the extremes of an unbalanced life.

Healthy intimacy can be received as love from God, our spouse, or close trusted friends. Each has different characteristics and will meet our needs if we respect the boundaries established by the designer of the system. We follow the same guidelines when giving validation to others by respecting limits and boundaries. Otherwise we will develop a dependence upon false sources, which will lead to unhealthy dependence and ultimately codependency. It is the same process of developing an addiction.

Another way people use their validation cards to cause problems is entering into relationships with no consideration for good boundaries. It is tragic, but the root cause may have been abuse or violence in their lives, which destroyed their sense of trust, especially if it was experienced as a child. The distinction between the first three validation cards will be blurred; they will lose their unique characteristics from being damaged. When this person grows up they are depending on something that cannot be trusted and will have difficulty in relationships wherever they go. If they do have a relationship with God, it will be tainted so that even their Salvation Card is damaged. These people think they need to please God through performance or perfectionism or He is going to pull their card and withdraw His love. They see God's love as conditional based on human experiences. Understanding our need for validation is not just a good idea, it can be critical for our own safety.

This is where recovery is at its best, because a person can surrender their set of cards and get help. Otherwise they will keep using the same cards over and over and over again, hoping that someday they will work. Healthy dependence on God and His principles needs to be established through surrender, but we know codependents will struggle to take that step. Without these changes mild codependents will become medium codependents, and eventually flaming codependents. Mildly dysfunctional people will become extremely dysfunctional. The progression of addiction will mirror the progression of codependency. *"All addicts are code-pendents, but not all are ready to accept it."*

A success story of repairing damaged cards took place with a pastor's wife in Russia. On one of the trips I took there, I was asked to speak with some people one-on-one. Through an interpreter I would listen to issues that people were struggling with and try to introduce them to some recovery principles that could help. It was a step of courage for this woman to seek assistance; it seems that false expectations of pastor's wives exist everywhere. She talked about feeling overwhelmed by being the mother of three boys and her role as the wife of the church leader. In her heart she wanted to be obedient to God and truly loved her family, so she could not understand her discouragement and lack of joy. She had been reading some information about codependency and it connected internally with how she was feeling, but the solutions were not working for her.

As we talked a couple of things became evident. One is that she felt obligated to a role of what she was "supposed to be" instead of what she was. She had some ideas about the definition of a good mother and wife based more on culture than the Bible. Another issue was having a passion in her heart for something in particular, but ignoring it because she felt guilty about not being a "good wife and mother" if she followed her heart. What this represented to me was a person who was trying to get validated through her lifestyle choices by using damaged cards instead of healthy ones. She was relying on the opinions of acquaintances and friends, depending on their approval but only getting criticism. Her "friends" told her that a good pastor's wife would not follow her own passion. "*That must have come from Proverbs 32:1, the scripture that doesn't exist.*" The irony was that her husband, the one who was the key source of intimacy in her life, actually supported her pursuing her passion. She was using the wrong cards at the wrong time. Basically, she was being a dysfunctional codependent, a mild one. External focus, trading good for bad, and living in the extremes.

So what was this passion that was such an issue? She wanted to be a Mary Kay Director. She had already started her business and loved the interaction with other women. She loved the products and the whole process of being a Mary Kay Consultant and wanted to excel, but she was obligated to a false sense of guilt and the opinions of others. It was interesting to watch her face light up when she talked about her business, and then watch it turn dark when she spoke of her obstacles. Her God-given personality was obviously people-oriented, and her codependency issues were crushing it. We discussed some simple tools to realign her thinking about what mattered most, setting boundaries with the opinions of others, and relying on the support of her husband for validation, removing the self-imposed condemnation that she thought was coming from God.

Six months later I returned to this same church on another mission trip to Russia. We arrived at the pastor's home for a meal and when we walked in I could tell something was different. She had a very joyful expression with the absence of stress that was present before. I was a little confused when she stood at attention next to her husband and they were both smiling. I was obviously supposed to be getting some message but was missing it, and then she pointed to the lapel of her blazer. There was a pin that recognized her as a Mary Kay Director. She had achieved her passion and was still a good mother and wife of a pastor.

While I was genuinely excited for her and her family, I could not help but think about how codependency robs people of their passion in life, and the destructive nature of seeking validation from the wrong sources. It was a real life lesson with a good outcome, one that required a shift from external sources to internal ones, correcting the truth about good and bad, and finding a balance between the extremes. When she started using the right validation cards at the right time with the right people, her codependency decreased and her fulfillment in life increased.

To take the next step in developing this analogy of validation cards and provide some direction on how to make changes, there also needs to be an example for people who have dependency all mixed up. This set of cards is called the "Dysfunctional Cards." There are only two cards in this set, which describes the state of a person before they make changes or get into recovery. People with this set of cards may not know their condition, an application of the layers of the onion. When the true condition is known, it might be hard to accept and the temptation will be to deny that it exists. Dismissing this condition or pretending it does not exist is pure denial. Shining the light of truth does not create what was hidden, it only reveals it. Some people are ready to see what is hidden, others are not. Hope exists for people who want the truth, regardless of how uncomfortable or painful it might be.

The first Dysfunctional Card is the "Mixed Up Card," which has all the same elements as the set of four healthy ones but on just one card. Everything is black and white; there is no distinction between the different types of validation, which represents a lack of good boundaries. Acquaintances can be intimate physically, emotionally, or spiritually, although all of these are reduced to insignificant levels. People like this will fall in love instantly and endlessly. Nice people with this condition will believe that if God brought two people together, at the same place, at the same time, then it must be for marriage, which is a codependent sense of emotions and spirituality. People who are living by their own set of rules have this card, whether they admit it or not. Humans cannot take God's principles, rearrange them to fit their own desires, and call them equal to or better than what God established. The Mixed Up Card also represents those who need to make decisions in their lives. *"Nothing remains the same; we progress in one direction or another, towards God or away from him."* People who recognize the confusion and make changes will avoid the pitfalls of addiction or codependency; otherwise they continue and increase the consequences. This describes a person who is headed for full-blown addiction or codependency but has not arrived there yet.

This one could also be viewed as a warning card. In soccer matches the referee can show the player a yellow card as a warning. It says something is going wrong, a violation of the rules has occurred. The player can object, argue, and plead their case as unfair, but the warning remains. The only possible way to avoid the next consequence is to change their attitude and behavior. People with a Mixed Up Card will have enough problems in their life to provide warning signs. Their efforts to get validation out of this world will have led to consequences already. They can blame, argue, and victimize themselves as much as they want, but the warning remains. If they do not change their attitude and behavior, there will be a progression to the next level.

The other Dysfunctional Card is the "Codependency Card," or for the addict the "Addiction Card." This is what people arrive at recovery or the cross of Christ with, when they hit bottom. Prior to that, validation comes from all the wrong sources. Codependents are addicted to negative emotions of anger, worry, control, and stress; some have affairs to meet their emotional needs. *"Codependency is an addiction to negative emotions."* It covers up, masks over, and keeps the real issues pushed down inside. Other codependents find solutions in prescription pills the same as addicts. This is the "you can have it all" card. It represents a person with no boundaries and a blur of emotions, those who struggle with relationships but blame everyone else and deny their part. The sad reality is when you meet people that are already in addiction recovery or church and are still getting validated with their Codependency Card. Not the ones who are changing their lives, but the ones who have been there for a while and are stuck in codependency. Chapter Two will describe many of their traits and character challenges.

The transformation from dysfunctional cards to healthy cards is a process that takes courage and time. Even people who are instantly delivered from an addiction have to work at their character flaws and learn new ways of living for God. Codependents are the same; when it comes to codependency, there are few if any testimonies of instant deliverance. There is, however, an abundance of examples from both men and women who are healing from codependency through the recovery process. This is where the award-winning series by Dr. Townsend and Dr. Cloud has had so much success in helping people with boundaries, which is a key component in overcoming codependency. Just like a lack of boundaries turns healthy cards into dysfunctional ones, establishing boundaries will transform dysfunctional cards into healthy ones. The blur becomes distinct, black and white transforms into color, and foolishness is replaced with wisdom. Moments of clarity replace periods of confusion.

Are you ready for pain? That is part of the process of healing. I had a conversation with a female friend in the church whose brother is a good friend of mine. He had a history of alcohol and drug abuse just like she did, but her brother left it all behind when he gave his life to Christ. His transformation came without recovery, but he challenged himself personally to grow in the grace and knowledge of Christ, and he became a solid example of a genuine

Christian man. The conversation with his sister took place several years into my recovery and her brother's Christian growth, while she was still struggling to stay clean and sober. She said, "I want what you have, what you and my brother have." Without hesitation I asked her, "Are you ready for pain?" She looked scared and shook her head to decline. I stated that she was not ready for what we had, because it came through the painful process of accepting truth and taking uncomfortable actions. Changing dysfunctional cards to healthy ones is not a "flash card" experience, which is just addictive thinking in the mind of the codependent by looking for a quick fix.

When people start recovery they have no idea what healthy cards look like. Codependency and addiction are similar in this regard because they result in a dysfunctional lifestyle. Recovery can repair damaged cards and restore them to healthy ones. The removal of character defects is the process of restoration that makes this possible.

This is where reconciliation comes into the equation. Without it there is no recovery. Relationships can be restored to health if the codependent is willing to be honest about the damage. This seems to be an issue for some codependents; they can easily see the need for an addict to make amends and reconcile their past, but have trouble seeing their own need to do the same. I have actually met people who were in recovery for their own codependency, and still could not see why their adult children wanted nothing to do with them. The adult children could clearly see that the problems still existed, mostly based on boundary violations like giving unwanted advice, still trying to control decisions, or being consumed with self-pity. I have also seen many examples where someone gets into addiction recovery and immediately wants to be reconciled to their family or adult children, which is actually an expression of codependency. They either demand or try to force reconciliation through passive manipulation, false guilt, or high expectations, all of which is void of Godly principles. They are trying to get validated through acceptance when they have not done enough yet to deserve it.

Rob E. #3 was a man who had this challenge. The only thing he talked about in recovery was getting back the relationship with his adult children. This was not a problem of addiction, but codependency. I tried to caution him to focus on his addiction issues and let his progress speak for itself to his children. He made an effort and everything went as planned for a while, but as soon as his children accepted him back into their lives he quit working on his recovery, relapsed, went to jail, and ruined everything. *"All addicts are codependents, but not all are ready to accept it."* His focus on validation was mixed up and codependent, and so were the results. He tried to gain access into his adult children's lives by using dysfunctional cards to get healthy results, like trying to fit a square peg in a round hole with a sledgehammer. Success will only cause damage.

There are also examples of people who followed directions, took ownership of their own recovery, made amends, and then waited for their adult children to choose to accept them back into their lives. These are the success stories, and they are amazing to watch. Once those relationships are reconciled, they usually stay that way because the person in recovery is giving and receiving validation in the proper way and from the right sources. These principles can transform lives, but only if they are properly applied. It typically requires a guide, someone who has gone through the experience of transforming his or her own cards. They are not emotionally enmeshed in the problem but know what it was like for them. They also know what is our responsibility and what is God's, and can help others who are mixed up and confused.

A girl who was attending the teenage recovery group at our church asked a question one day about why her father could not give her the love and affection she so desperately wanted. I knew the family well and tried to think of a way to explain it. I told her, *"You can't get spring water from a muddy well."* She wanted validation from a source that could not provide it. Her father was still living with a set of dysfunctional cards and she wanted him to have healthy ones. The irony was that she was beginning to grow and establish healthy boundaries, and develop a personal relationship with God. She did not have to wait for someone else to go first. Our ability to grow and become healthy is never forced under the influence of another person. We have the choice to change our lives, unless codependency takes it away. Families do not have to wait for the addict to get clean and sober, addicts do not have to wait for the family to see their own problems. God is the ultimate source of strength to overcome addiction or codependency, and he uses people who have already experienced transformed lives to help others do the same. Our part is to make sure we are going to the right source.

This is where people get stuck who are not willing to take the next step, such as those in recovery who need to participate in a program for secondary issues of codependency, or those in church who are avoiding these issues behind a wall of repetitive religious activities. They keep dropping the bucket in the well and can't figure out why they keep getting muddy water, so they just keep doing the same thing over and over expecting a different result. Nothing will change until they accept the truth and move to the right source.

A benefit of codependent recovery is learning to respond instead of reacting, and the work environment can be the best place to practice this principle. There was a certain supervisor in the plant where I worked that seemed to enjoy getting angry. We had a lot of interaction from my role in the maintenance department, and none of it was good. As much as I did not like his hostility, I also could not seem to keep from reacting to it. But my newfound principles of recovery for codependency said that I could respond instead and not get pulled into arguments. I developed an internal tool that was simple: imagining a line drawn between myself and the other person. All that was allowed on my side were my problems and things I was personally responsible for or otherwise it stayed on the other side of the line. It took some practice to make this work.

One day I got called out to fix something that was broken, and this supervisor was waiting for me to arrive. He began yelling insults and profanity at me directly, in front of a lot of other people. With each of his statements I made a conscious decision: was it on my side of the line or not? One rude comment after another, with each threat and insult I would internally say "no," "not mine," "no," and so on. It was obvious that he wanted to argue, but I was not even getting upset because all the anger and hostility was his. I "chose" not to let it cross the line and become my problem, and was responding instead of reacting just by using a simple tool. This did not mean that I was silently standing there taking the insults, or that I was enjoying the experience, but the things I said were not reactions to his anger. When he finally had enough he stormed away and I fixed the equipment. My Dysfunctional Cards were being transformed into Healthy Cards, because I was going to the right source, listening to those with experience, taking responsibility for the actions, and trusting God for the results. It was working. Primary recovery did not produce results for the secondary issues. Christianity can actually increase dysfunctional living for the codependent. Defiance, confusion, and denial are part of the problem, just a bucket of muddy water.

The episode with the supervisor in the plant was another personal milestone in my codependent recovery, because as I made the repairs I was calm and peaceful inside. Not by just trying to control emotions, but having a sense of internal boundaries with the ability to choose what I would accept and reject, exactly what God wanted me to do in all areas of my life. I did not have to leave the job, wait for someone else to change, or just keep showing up and being frustrated. I also didn't have to play the victim role or demand entitlement, neither of which would have produced change for my codependency. People who run to play the victim role remain unchanged; they are externally focused and will only increase their codependency. If I had played the victim I would have missed the growth, and anything gained would have been worthless in comparison to the value of healing and change that came from adversity.

A while later one of the other supervisors told me that I just wasn't fun anymore, that they enjoyed it when I was easy to get upset. Another moment of clarity, having to accept the truth that I had been providing free entertainment for dysfunctional people. I could have let that be a source of irritation, but when he said this I just laughed, at myself. When I thought I had been in control, I was not. When I accepted my weaknesses, took the right action, and trusted God for the results, then I had what I was really looking for.

Recovery from codependency can be empowering, but as with addiction recovery we have to surrender to win. Once these changes are established in one area of our lives, they can be used in all other areas. The circumstances that push these issues to the surface are rarely the only ones in our lives where codependency exists. Just like addiction, just like the hanging mobile, just like attempts to get validated, the line between addiction and codependency is self-imposed. *"All addicts are codependents, and all codependents are addicts, but not all are ready to accept it."*

Are you ready for pain?

2

Personal Titles of Codependents

The way codependency is expressed has so many different forms, it is impossible to describe using only a few terms. The list can be so extensive that it can be exhausting and make it difficult for people to identify with the descriptions. Therefore, twelve titles have been chosen for each of the categories of flaming and mild in order to provide useful and practical information that will allow people to find their own codependent traits. Medium codependents are in the transition from mild to flaming as their issues evolve. Their character traits will change as the codependency progresses. None of these are intended to be exhaustive, since some could be a complete study all on their own. These personal titles are intended to make the information simple to recall, especially in a crisis or when the internal pull towards old habits is strong. Some are amusing, others are not — it may depend on how severe each person's codependency is. All of them can be male or female.

Each of these descriptions has multiple applications but with common characteristics; therefore, examples and analogies will provide a way to understand and apply them. Consistent with the general theme throughout this book is the idea that flaming codependents need more of a direct impact to accept truth, whereas mild codependents would be injured by such an approach. The titles listed for each category take this into account. Titles used for flaming codependents may be hard to read and accept, mild ones a bit easier. What matters most is honesty when reviewing them and to pick the ones that apply to you as an individual.

There may be times that you recognize someone else's title. If so, use that information to gain understanding and wisdom, not to set someone straight or help them see the errors of their ways. This information is best used as a mirror for self-examination, not a magnifying glass to look at the faults of others. This principle was taught by Jesus and recorded in the Matthew 7:1-3 when he said, *"Why do you look at the speck of sawdust in your brother's eye and pay no attention to the plank in your own eye? How can you say to your brother, 'Let me take the speck out of your eye,' when all the time there is a plank in your own eye? You hypocrite, first take the plank out of your own eye, and then you will see clearly to remove the speck from your brother's eye."* If the information helps you to better understand someone else, then use that insight properly.

This chapter is really about the problem of codependency. Chapters Three through Five will provide many of the solutions, thereby taking the next step in healing through looking at core issues. Recovery is often referred to as the process of peeling an onion, one layer at a time. It is the journey inward where true healing and growth take place. Trying to cut to the core without carefully peeling the layers away will only cause damage. Acceptance and identification of the problem always comes before the solution can be used; otherwise what are you really solving? People who want to bypass this process are still struggling with pride and denial. They either want a quick fix or are just looking for reasons to blame someone else for their problems. So, before focusing on solutions, let's look at some analogies of the common problems.

12 Titles of Mild Codependents

The Collector

Real collectors look for items of value. They are interested in finding things that would be worth obtaining. A good one will invest time in learning how to separate the good from the bad. Codependent Collectors on the other hand are pretty much junk collectors. They look for opportunities to obtain things most people would avoid, mainly other people's problems. This type of codependent invests very little time in taking care of their own issues, but plenty of time focusing externally and getting involved in situations they have no business being a part of. Their identity depends on collecting lots of junk from other people.

Think about the idea of a "hoarder," someone who collects things to the extreme. These people are struggling with some type of problem or dysfunctional behavior. Their physical houses will be cluttered with items they don't need and should get rid of. The same is true of the codependent Collector, but more in the emotional and spiritual sense. They have typically collected so much junk that it has become a personal health problem. People with this codependent issue will never be healthy until they stop and take an honest look in the mirror. Their dependence on other people's problems is just a way to avoid their own.

Another version of this codependent trait is to be a garbage Collector, which is someone who simply collects items that would not even be classified as junk. They are the ones who repeat the action of cleaning up the messes left by other people, or in some cases actually letting other people bring the mess over to their house. Examples are parents who keep paying their children's bills and debts, even when the child is in their 30's or 40's. A codependent will defend this practice by asking what is wrong with helping out a child who is in need, which would be fine if it was the first or second time, but not when it has become a lifestyle.

Life has enough personal challenges on its own without adding other people's problems. The fine line between helping and enabling is the challenge for the Collector. Serving other people in a healthy manner is the equivalent of being a good collector, knowing when to invest and when to let go. A codependent Collector has trouble telling the difference, and will turn their service into a health hazard. Just deciding not to collect emotional and spiritual junk is usually not enough, at least not until the obstacles are removed.

The Lifeguard

Lifeguards at a pool or beach have a valuable job to do: save the lives of people who are in danger. Codependent Lifeguards are those who rescue people that are capable of saving themselves, ones who like to play the role of a helpless person. This type of codependency typically shows up in parents when dealing with their children's problems, or spouses that make excuses for their partner that are actually lies. It is a mild form of codependency that comes from not understanding how to help others without enabling.

The basic problem for this type of codependent is that their role requires someone who needs to be rescued, but as we already know if you *"rescue them, and you will have to do it again."* Proverbs 19:19. Codependent Lifeguards who do not quit or retire will eventually become Expectant Parents, and the consequences of their actions will graduate from mild to flaming. *"Going the extra mile for someone is a short term event, not a lifestyle."* Lifeguards will never experience change as long as they see themselves as someone who needs to rescue others. Ultimately they are playing God in the lives of other people, and need to stop.

In the classic movie "The Sandlot," one of the boys known as "Squints" makes a daring move to be rescued by the beautiful young female lifeguard. Squints pretends to be drowning, and is rescued by the lifeguard where he receives mouth-to-mouth resuscitation. But his plot is exposed when she realizes he was just stealing a kiss. He is quickly escorted to the exit and is not allowed to return. What do you think would have happened if Squints tried a similar stunt again a week or so later? If he had even made it to the pool, the lifeguard would have responded differently knowing that he could not be trusted.

Codependent Lifeguards continue to rescue people even though it is not the first time. The level of common sense that would prevent a real lifeguard from being fooled does not exist. They will repeat the rescue over and over, expecting a different result each time. Until they break the cycle and apply Biblical truth there is no hope for the Lifeguard to make good decisions. The one who was rescued will keep trying as long as it continues to work. One addict tried to fake an overdose by collapsing on the front lawn, apparently unconscious. He was caught with drugs at home and needed a way out. Surrounded by a family of codependent Lifeguards, the call went out to 911. The siren could be heard as the ambulance got closer and when it turned the corner by the house, the addict jumped up and ran away. He was exposed. For a healthy family that would have been the last straw, but it wasn't. Codependent Lifeguards do what they do best just continue to rescue.

The Helper

This type of codependent will help you whether you need it or not. It is listed as a mild form because most people with this type of problem are not trying to hurt people; they want to help but lack good boundaries. While meeting with a group to discuss a drug problem, I addressed a challenging question to one of the family members, and another family member answered for them (both were middle-aged siblings). When I pointed out what just happened they were both surprised. Evidently it had been that way all of their lives. In fact, it was a humorous moment in our discussion that we all laughed at.

Codependent Helpers just need to learn some boundaries in the areas of giving, whether advice, time, or money. If not, they will eventually become any one of several flaming codependents. It is unfortunate that Helpers get taken advantage of by people who are needy. If the codependent cannot see their part of the problem and correct it, they will eventually quit helping or continue doing so in the wrong way. One man who was working with me to help addicts had to face this issue head-on when someone we had both spent a lot of time with relapsed on heroin. When he was expressing his discouragement about this addict I told him, *"There's only one way to prevent this from ever happening again, just don't help anyone."* If we go to extremes just because codependency could exist in helping others, then we will never find the balance in our service to God. Just like other forms of codependency, we will quit or burn out. To stay out of extremes and serve in a healthy balance, we do what we can to help people without expectation, and leave the results in God's hands. People who find it difficult to establish these boundaries will find the ability to do so by addressing their own codependency.

The Chameleon

" *In God's incredible creation there are animals that can change their appearance to adapt to any circumstances. People are not one of them."* But that does not stop codependent Chameleons from trying, because they need to adapt to the external world to establish their identity.

Have you ever met a person that has done everything you have and more? No matter what you mention, by the end of the conversation they have either done the same thing or did it better than you. Another characteristic is telling someone about your health struggles and before you know it they have the same illness. These people can also be referred to as "hypochondriacs," but for the purpose of codependency we need a broader description, since the same characteristic exist outside of medical issues.

This is actually the distortion of an attribute God wants us to have, that of being able to adapt to different environments for the purpose of sharing the gospel. The apostle Paul understood the value of this ability when he wrote, *"I have become all things to all people so that by all possible means I might save some. I do all this for the sake of the gospel, that I may share in its blessings."* I Corinthians 9:22-23. Codependency will reverse the roles and turn this asset into a liability, causing people who lack their own identity to take on whatever is around them. They will be ineffective in carrying a message of hope that is based on truth, because the personality of the messenger is based on confusion. Those who are receiving the message will pick up on the inconsistency, and wonder how the messenger has anything to offer them. We don't wait for perfection to share the message of hope in Jesus Christ, but we also do not pretend to be something we are not.

Codependent Chameleons are externally focused people in a constantly changing world. Personal identity is evasive. We can adapt to different situations in life without changing on the inside, unless people pleasing is a problem. Then we will have to say and do things that are intended to make everyone happy, an impossible goal. As the conditions change around the Chameleon, they will change to adapt.

The Good Wife

A classic example of codependency is a woman who remains faithful to her husband in a dysfunctional relationship. He treats the marriage as an opportunity to have a clean house, food on the table, clean clothes, and plenty of time for activities related to his interest. Christian women who want to be viewed by the world as "faithful" will tolerate this type of treatment and not recognize their own codependency. Even when the husband's hobbies or job become more important than the family, the Good Wife will just go along with the program because she wants to be seen as, well, a good wife.

These codependents are often afraid of making changes because it might result in a divorce, so at best they make a marginal effort to address the problems. A marriage that is driven to the brink of divorce because a problem actually gets addressed is not God's definition for marriage, where *"they are no longer two, but one flesh. Therefore what God has joined together, let no one separate."* Mark 10:8-9. When role reversal turns God's plan for marriage into a relationship that is extreme and out of balance, where only one person is working at the union, it will never become a loving dependent relationship.

An extreme example I came across many years ago was a woman whose husband was living somewhere else. She suspected he had a drug problem and was having an affair, but he was bringing his laundry by and she was washing it for him. In a phone call she asked if I thought that was a problem because she wanted to be a faithful spouse and keep hope alive for the marriage. Just another example of how codependency can blind people to the truth. Being a good wife is defined by what a person is on the inside and healthy actions, not by tolerating external circumstances just to look good. Professional counseling is often needed in these situations.

Men can also have this problem, wanting to be seen as "faithful" in difficult circumstances. While this would definitely be character strength, it makes no sense when the wife has already left the marriage with no intention of returning. Men with codependency will imagine that, when it's all over, they will be held in the highest regard by other people because they remained faithful to a person that was anything but faithful. A more likely explanation is that the man is deeply wounded and is tolerating inappropriate by their spouse, just to save their own image. Even if the motives are good which is the case in some situations, codependency will ruin any chance to make the right decisions. If you run clean water through a dirty filter you will only get dirty water. You can't get spring water from a muddy well.

The Paramedic

What incredible service paramedics provide the community. They may not be full-scale doctors, but they can be really good at what they do. Good paramedics know and accept their limitations. But the codependent Paramedic does not know their own limits and tries to be a cure for all hurts. Many pastors and clergy struggle with this issue because they have so many people that come to them with problems, and they truly want to help everyone. Just like real paramedics, clergy need to know their limits or they will become dysfunctional in their attempts to help people. Leaving the ministry or burning out is often the result.

Another characteristic of this type of codependency is trying to diagnose problems that a person has no experience with. Doctors can diagnose conditions that paramedics cannot. Through a lack of healthy boundaries, codependent Paramedics will provide a diagnosis free of charge, even when it's beyond their ability to do so. A common example is when the family or friends of an addict think they can fix the problem through enough love or support, when they really don't understand addiction in the first place. Codependents will have a hard time seeing when the situation is beyond their ability. Those who truly want to retire from being codependent Paramedics typically do so by reaching the end of their abilities, accepting their limitations, and asking for help. Proper wisdom can produce proper results, just as a lack of wisdom can produce tragic results. The best approach for a codependent Paramedic is to be honest about their own level of skills in whatever the environment is, whether work, family, or dealing with an addiction.

The Translator

Good translators have skills that are valuable in communication. It goes beyond just knowing the languages being spoken, and includes knowing when to speak and when to listen. Codependent Translators lack those skills; they just like to interpret everything based on what they think. They are not good listeners but do like to speak, and the only language they know is their own. You can tell someone has this type of codependency when they say, "Oh, so you're saying that (insert wrong interpretation)." This will come up especially if the codependent's attitude or behavior is being addressed as a problem. Translators are good at avoidance.

Another example is when a codependent Translator hears what someone says, but determines that it is not really what they meant. When someone states what they like or do not like, the Translator will correct the error because they believe they know better. Controlling types of codependents will have this trait, and will be intrusive with their opinions and dominating personalities. Children are often the targets of the codependent Translator. The ability to make age-appropriate decisions is taken away by this type of codependent. It can also be expressed as a problem of being a "know-it-all," because nobody really knows it all.

Translators are always ready to correct an error. There are times when people say things with the best of intentions and make mistakes in what they say. It's just part of being human. A codependent Translator will never let this slide, because they have to make sure that the other person is fully aware of their mistake, especially if there is an audience. Ego and pride are core issues for Translators.

This type of person can be a "problem solver" as well. When you talk with them they are not listening, just thinking of how they are going to tell you to solve the problem. Men have this trait in marriages, when they don't understand their wife is telling them about a problem just to talk about it, not to receive a solution. This can be a startling revelation to some men. Besides, any man who thinks he can accurately translate his wife's intentions while at the same time being a codependent Translator has missed the mark completely. Better to learn to listen without translating, otherwise known as "active listening."

The Tornado

Most people know what a "tornado" is; some have experienced them first hand while others just through pictures and video images. Scientific study of this type of storm has resulted in understanding that all tornadoes are not the same. According to the National Severe Storm Laboratory (NSSL), there are basically two types of tornadoes. One is a "super-cell," which produces the more destructive storms. The other is a "non super-cell," which generates several types of tornadoes that are less intense. According to the NSSL, "scientists are not sure how strong they are, but they tend to be small." Land-spouts and waterspouts are included in this category of small storms, yet even these can pull elements that are close by into the funnel.

Codependent Tornadoes tend to be like land-spouts, whirling around without causing major damage. People can tend to be afraid of them and try to classify all of them as the destructive type. However, the codependent Tornado really only has one purpose, to pull others into the storm. They tend to be a nice person who most of the time moves along like a summer breeze. But when the conditions of life stir up the atmosphere, a codependent can form into a Tornado that begins to spin. As they gain speed and strength, the goal is to get other people who are close by into the middle of the storm.

Rob E. #2 is a codependent Tornado. His job has periods of time where everything is smooth and moves along without stress. But there are also times when circumstances create a much higher level of demands. This is when Rob E. #2 becomes a Tornado. He will enter the presence of other people like a small storm that is spinning, because he needs other people to get pulled into the middle. One of the ways you can tell this type of codependent is by one of the statements they make; "I don't need this" is a commonly used phrase. But the truth is they do need it, because the codependent Tornado is practicing avoidance. At first this might seem confusing, but not when you consider how often and under what circumstances the storm appears. It's a predictable pattern. The circumstances might be random, but the reaction to them is the same. The codependent Tornado is a storm waiting to happen. All they need is a reason to spin.

We all know this type of person; they will call on phone or show up in a panic. They want others to believe that the situation was beyond their control, but most people with this tendency actually fail to take action when they had ample opportunity to plan. People will wait until the last minute to take action, and when the circumstances produce a crisis they will get others involved. Most codependent Tornadoes are efficient in how they pull others into the funnel, and if you're not careful you will suddenly be sucked in. Even people who have experience with this type of person can let their guard down and before they know it they are saying to themselves, "They got me again." What the codependent Tornado needs are some "storm chasers," and they often know right where to find them because they are the same ones that got pulled in during the last storm.

In the other extreme, this same person will move from aggressive to passive, but their need to get others involved remains. Instead of spinning they will become more like a storm with a low-level depression, one that moves slowly. It's a mild version of being a victim, which can happen when everything falls apart. They will become needy for help, but will pull others in by making statements to gain sympathy. The portrait of this codependent will be a person with both palms up and a sad look on their face, as if to say, "What can I do?" But the really sad part is that whether passive or aggressive, spinning or depressed, this person will never get out of their own storm until they face their own codependency.

The Blues Singer

A really good blues singer can set the mood around them. Their talent and ability to communicate the message through music is extraordinary. There are other people who have the same talent, but it is tainted with codependency and is not music to anyone's ears. The codependent Blues Singer will talk endlessly about what is wrong with life and the world in general. I heard an adult Christian say once that "life is hard and then you die," a genuine codependent Blues Singer.

These are mild codependents that are not trying to hurt anyone, but they have a tendency to pull others down with their negativity. Musicians like to have an audience, and so does this type of codependent. They have creative ways to communicate the message, subtle comments about the way things used to be, or shaking their heads about where the world is headed. For them, the world is always headed in a bad direction, and the past was always better than the present. They will talk about the good old days and how it is just a shame the way things are now. Codependent Blues Singers would do well to study history, because the only time the world was better was before sin entered, and the next time will be when God creates a new heaven and a new earth. Until then, history will repeat itself, and we can choose how we view the world around us. This type of person depends on the negative side of life to give them a reason to avoid looking at themselves. The truth is the problems of the world actually do exist, within them.

This type of codependent over time will become a Killer Poodle (Flaming codependent analogy). They can be fooled by their passive nature in expressing negativity, but a more aggressive expression is waiting to raise its ugly head. If they are able to remain a codependent Blues Singer for a long time, the avoidance will come from other people who just don't want to hear it anymore. Depression, loneliness, and poor mental health await this person. An "attitude of gratitude" will go a long way in correcting this condition.

The Private Investigator

Investigators are people who search for facts that will lead to the truth. The typical picture of a private investigator is one who works alone to solve a mystery, the subject of many television series and movies. The codependent Private Investigator also likes to work alone, because they are on a mission: to prove they are right. They suspect everyone else, and will adapt to whatever method is needed to get to the bottom of the situation. Some see themselves as detectives, maybe a spy, and still others as commandos, but all of it is based on fantasy. What they believe to be the truth will eventually be found, or so they think.

The basic problem for this codependent is trust. For some reason their past has left them with the condition of not trusting other people, and their codependency will not allow them to develop trust within close personal relationships. If this type of person has experienced infidelity by a former spouse, they will have trouble trusting the faithfulness of another person. Without change this person will become a flaming codependent Projector.

One codependent Christian woman with this problem actually withheld sexual relations from her husband, and then used it as a basis to suspect him of having an affair. She was sure that the truth was going to come out and kept an eye out for evidence, which only lead to misinterpreting what she saw. It was impossible for her to be a codependent Private Investigator and have a loving dependent relationship at the same time. The irony is that her husband was a Deacon in the church, a respected man who was faithful to his wife. Men with this condition will become the strong silent type as a defense from being hurt. They will act like the lead character in an old spy movie, with few words and a lot of stern looks.

Codependent Private Investigators can be like human wiretaps, trying to be clever at how they get their information. I was talking with a man, who developed an addiction problem, and during our conversation on the phone I heard someone else quietly make a comment in the background, and then he repeated the comment. It turned out to be his wife who was listening in and telling him what to say. The conversation ended quickly and he was asked to call back when he was alone. The Private Investigator needed to be cut off from the surveillance so that we could move forward.

People with this type of codependency will sabotage their current relationships, sometimes based on past experiences. Thinking they are protecting themselves from being deceived, or making sure their version of the truth is known, they are actually destroying any chance for genuine love. A person who is suspicious will not trust, and one who is protected from hurt cannot love. They work alone, and they get what they work for: isolation. *"There is pain without love, but there is no love without pain,"* something a codependent Private Investigator will never understand.

The Drone

The idea of a drone has become commonplace with the development of units for the general public. The average citizen can buy an inexpensive one or a high performance model. The best feature is the ability to take pictures or video from up in the air, a unique view that is provided by the drone. The commercial ones are not dangerous, but military drones are capable of much, much more.

Codependent Drones also have a unique characteristic, one that is much older than the new technology. It originates with their spiritual condition, but bleeds over into their mental and emotional abilities. They believe they have a special view of the world around them that is not available to everyone else. Simply put, they have their heads stuck in the clouds. A common description is when someone is "so heavenly-minded that they are no earthly good." Having spiritual discernment is an asset that every Christian should strive for, but a person who is already codependent will struggle with developing this ability and will arrive at a false destination. They depend more on themselves than on God, but will be convinced otherwise.

Rose E. #5 is a codependent Drone. She is a Christian woman who has some very strange ideas about life that are all based on a hyper-spiritual focus. As a codependent, her life is a trail of dysfunctional wreckage: a broken marriage, no income, and single parent of several children who have severe behavioral problems. Many people sought to help her, but when meeting with the only thing that mattered was whether or not they were Christians. Nothing else mattered, nothing. When my wife and I spoke with her, she said that she was going to move to a place where they had apartments with tennis courts, a swimming pool, and a gymnasium for her kids. We asked where this incredible place was. She said it was out there somewhere. When asked how she would afford it her only reply was "The Lord will provide." Genuine faith in God's provision is real, placing trust in our Heavenly Father is the right thing to do, but hiding behind faith as a way of falsely believing that God will provide your own custom utopia is wrong. Several people who genuinely tried to help her eventually just walked away confused or frustrated. She just never seemed to have her feet planted on the earth, but her head was definitely in the clouds. In her own understanding, she believed her perspective was higher than other people, when in fact it was the opposite.

Just like other forms of codependency, this condition can cause problems not only for the person but also affects the lives of those who are close by. For that reason this may be on the border between mild and medium, but most people with this condition are not as extreme as Rose E. #5. The mild type of codependent Drone can make some simple adjustments, ones that may just require an honest person to help bring them back to reality. At the same time others may resemble the military type of drone that is capable of destruction. Codependent Drones often resist change until life brings them to their knees, which places their feet firmly on the earth. A reality check, one that might actually improve their spiritual awareness.

The Whac-a-Mole

In the 1970's a game was invented that become known as the Whac-a-Mole. It was about the size of a pinball machine but had a flat surface with holes in it. The player had a rubber mallet that was used to hit the fake moles when they popped up out of the holes. The challenge was that they moved quickly, disappearing and popping up in another location, so you had to chase them. As the game continued the speed of the moles increased, making it a wild and crazy game. Whether we ever played the game or not, we have all met a codependent Whac-a-Mole.

This type of person plays out their codependent game in the way they communicate about a problem. When you have to address a problem about them, and get close to the truth, they will quickly change the point of the discussion. If you try to get refocused they will speed up and change faster. One of their favorite phrases is "Oh yeah, well what about you?" This is why they will eventually become a codependent Projector still using the same phrase. Anything the Whac-a-Mole can bring up is a legitimate part of the subject to them, nothing is off limits. Conversations become more of a speed game of misdirection than healthy communication. You have to chase them through a subject and the response is always the quickest and most compulsive reaction they can come up with. It's all about avoidance and never about acceptance. They are focusing externally, so if you get too close to the internal problem, they will need to shift, become evasive, and keep changing.

So, how do you form a loving dependent relationship with a person like this? Simply put, you don't. It is a life of loneliness, because people get tired of playing the game and either leave or just stop communicating. Isolation might not happen right away — the mild codependent nature of this person can be tolerated for some time — but it will come. Without change the codependent wins, and everyone loses. A Whac-a-Mole never changes; day after day it is just the same game, over, and over, and over.

12 Titles of Flaming Codependents

The Expectant Parent

When a mother is expecting the delivery of her baby we refer to her as an Expectant Mother. She has great anticipation of the child that is to come, eagerly awaiting the arrival through birth. When the baby is born a different phase of development begins, one that will continue to change and evolve for the rest of the lives of the child and the parents. Age-appropriate decisions will gradually be transferred to the child, but not for the child of the Expectant Parent. Their role depends on the child remaining a child, which is an expression of codependency.

This title goes to the person who never moves beyond infancy in their own parenting skills. The children eventually become teenagers or adults, but the parents are still behaving as though the children were babies. They are stuck in the routine of being eternal paternal parents. Could you imagine what it would be like if a child never developed physically? If they remained as infants years after birth? We would call that a disability or a developmental problem. It is the same for the codependent when children are not allowed to grow up emotionally, mentally, and spiritually. Parents with this form of codependency do well while the children are very young, but when parenting becomes a struggle that requires teaching maturity, they are lost and would rather go back to a time when the kids were young. They need the joy of the expectant mother to continue, simply because it feels better and does not require maturity.

The most likely the source of the Expectant Parent's codependency is their own childhood, where they learned the traits that are now being passed on to their children. A common form of violation occurs in making decisions, because the children are not allowed to make them even when they should. People can fall into the trap of believing everything was better when the expectation of parenthood existed, or when the infant depended so much on being taken care of. Fathers can have the all the same tendencies as mothers in these situations. Expectant Parents have a very difficult time letting their children grow up.

Rose E. #7 was raised in church and has been a Christian all her life. She was also raised by a severely codependent mother who controlled all the decision making in the lives of her four children. One day, mom decided that there had not been enough activity at the altar in church, so that Sunday morning she informed all of her children that they were going to "get saved." This meant that the children would go forward after the worship service and declare that they had all accepted Jesus into their hearts, in front of the whole church. We could easily describe this as spiritual abuse, a false celebration of the Gospel, but at least it made mom happy.

Disagreeing was not an option; children of Expectant Parents do what they are told because the choice to refuse is not available, or refusal could bring out the wrath of the parent. So these children did what they were told, but when Rose E. #7 talked about it as an adult it was not with respect or joy from the occasion, it was with fierce resentment towards her mother. Expectant Parents are conduits of generational dysfunction, also called codependency. Rose E. #7 was in recovery for her own codependency and was working through the process of growing up emotionally, mentally, and spiritually. She was learning how to allow her own children to mature, and it was a joy to watch her grow and break the cycle of codependency. A gradual process that required commitment and consistency, but it was changing a generational curse into a blessing for her own children.

The Bible gives us a description of the spiritual process that takes place when we are born of the Spirit; in John 3 Jesus called it being "born again." The Apostle Paul wrote about a comparison between being born again and remaining as an infant. I Corinthians 3:1-3 states, *"Brothers and sisters, I could not address you as people who live by the Spirit but as people who are still worldly, mere infants in Christ. I gave you milk, not solid food, for you were not yet ready for it. Indeed, you are still not ready."* This description of spiritual infancy is the same problem that is produced when parents do not let their babies grow up. When these children physically become adults they will still be like infants who cannot digest solid truth. Their world is built on the illusion that relationships are based on controlling other people. Without genuine Christianity or recovery they will simply pass the problem along to the next generation.

Children raised under these circumstances rarely know what boundaries are, and if they do they are constantly pushing the limits and getting mad if they do not get their way. We see this type of child all the time; they are in their late teens or mid-20's and still throwing fits like a young child. Their parents are frustrated because they expect the adult child to somehow act like a mature adult, when the truth is they never learned how. Maturing is a process that happens over time, not an event that takes place on your 18th birthday.

One of the ways Expectant Parents continue this process is to manage the finances of an adult child who is old enough to do it for himself. The typical picture is a child in their mid-20's who has made a mess with their finances and cannot even be trusted to get a paycheck and be responsible with it. Examples are when the parent holds onto the checkbook, deposits the paychecks for them, or perhaps pays the bills and only gives the child enough cash for a short period of time. Somehow this is supposed to induce financial responsibility into the irresponsible child. Only a codependent could come to that conclusion, because this is really more about the Expectant Parent than it is the child. While the excuse is given that it is helping to save the child from financial harm, is it not really about the fear of the parent? This is another characteristic of Expectant Parents; they point to the external circumstances as the reason for their behavior, when the truth is it comes from avoidance of internal issues. So what is the real problem? Simply put, *"it's easier to enable someone than experience the pain of letting go."* When a codependent is faced with making a decision that means letting go of control or trying to influence the outcome, it is much easier to enable and avoid all the potential fear or discomfort. The drug of choice for this codependent is avoidance, and it works.

This parent can also be the type of person that does not listen or follow directions, but expects everyone else to do so. They argue a lot and develop an attitude of believing they are unique and no one else understands. This is the secondary application to this title, having high expectations of others that can never be satisfied. The Expectant Parent wants everything done their way, which is just another sign of immaturity since they believe their way is the only way. They have high expectations of others that are coming from a person who lacks genuine respect. When it does not work out their way, they usually just raise the expectations. Never satisfied, never good enough, critical of others. Men with this problem will say, "If you want a job done right you have to do it yourself," which is just an excuse for not being able to trust or teach another person. It is a codependent statement for the purpose of role reversal and focusing externally, because no one could ever meet the high expectations of this type of codependent.

There is one version of the Expectant Parent that will further complicate the issue: being a stepparent. Controlling mothers or fathers who try to exert their influence over stepchildren without having the maturity to do so will multiply the problems. Some try to force the children to call them "mother" or "father," others demand respect while giving none. If the children are teenagers and the codependent parent is still using methods best suited for an infant, there will be trouble. An Expectant Parent whose ideas are out of touch with reality will focus externally and blame the children, or have an emotional break down and blame everyone. Either way nothing will change until the expectations and maturity of the stepparent changes, a journey inward not outward.

Healing from the effects of being an Expectant Parent takes time, but to quote a common recovery cliché, "when nothing changes, then nothing changes."

The Killer Poodle

What a picture this paints. The cute, adorable, and cuddly creature that will take a bite out of you with its sharp teeth. This title is for a flaming codependent because of the way they hurt others. Most of the Killer Poodle's character comes from trying to control the uncontrollable. They spend a lot of time and energy pushing their agenda in other people's lives. The natural outcome is frustration, anger, and sometimes rage. These people are polite, calm, and helpful, until you disagree with them or point out their inappropriate behavior. Then you better watch out, because they will turn hostile and abusive. Killer Poodles run between two extremes — it is all-cute or none, all passive or full attack.

Rose E. #8 was a kind and considerate lady in church. She liked to help others, especially when it involved giving advice. Her family consisted of a compliant spouse and a child who became an alcoholic. Several attempts by the adult child to achieve sobriety failed, each one bringing more of Rose E. #8's Killer Poodle instincts to bear on the family. Long lectures, admonishing, and ridicule were tools used to help the adult child see the problem clearly. She was always kind to me personally, never a harsh word, until one day when I suggested that she might need to focus on her own issues. Then the teeth came out, along with the rage and extremely aggressive language. It was hard to believe that it was the same person. It was then that I finally understood her husband's nature. He was always very quiet when she was around, but would talk non-stop when she was not. Seems he had been bit one too many times and learned to keep quiet as a survival skill.

Dependence in relationships that are out of control will produce this kind of codependent problem. The codependent continually develops their character flaws through relationships. People do not remain the same over time; codependents without recovery eventually become Killer Poodles. Remember, we were created in God's image for loving dependent relationships. How people are currently is not how they have always been. If we could see them at a younger age we would see a different person, probably one that had a chance to change but did not. After a while codependency can turn even a good person into an old dog that just bites people. What is important to this codependent is that the external world sees them as kind and considerate of others, meanwhile they keep the teeth hidden.

Maybe these traits were learned growing up, perhaps developed over time during adulthood, but most likely a combination of both. The irony of Killer Poodles is that they are often people pleasers looking for affirmation, and since no one can please everyone there has to be an expression of failure. Codependents who are Killer Poodles swing back and forth between pity and rage, contentment and frustration. They are living a life of extreme contradiction that can never be satisfied.

The Christian church is an organization that attracts Killer Poodles. There is affirmation to be received for service, an atmosphere that can bring kindness and compassion. Volunteers are always needed, so codependents have easy access to responsibility. A healthy person who serves for the proper reasons with the proper motives will do well in good times and bad. But this type of codependent will only do well when things are good. When struggles come they will be territorial with their area of service, by trying to establish control and dominance. If you keep proper respect it will be all-cute and smiles, if you cross the line you will get bit.

Rarely are there any areas of service in the church that are led in isolation. God's plan for the church is to be the body of Christ, having many members and parts that work together for a common cause. *"For just as each of us has one body with many members, and these members do not all have the same function, so in Christ we, though many, form one body, and each member belongs to all the others."* Romans 12:4-5. When a function or project in the church requires members of the body to work together is when you find out who the Killer Poodles are. At first everything will go well, cooperation and support will come in abundance. But codependents of this type have a pre-determined plan of how things are going to work out, so the goal is to just get everyone else on board.

The degree of codependency for a Killer Poodle will determine when they get irritated, and when they bite. The limit is different for each person and over time it will happen more quickly. The one thing all Killer Poodles have in common is that when attention is focused on them personally as being a problem, they react with vengeance. To accept criticism would be to admit something is wrong, and cannot happen. Killer Poodles are probably the most destructive kind of codependent because of the way they hurt other people. Recovery from this condition most often requires help from a professional counselor.

The Projector

Using the analogy of a movie projector we can understand how some codependents express themselves. Projectors are literally externally focused; they take what is on the inside and project an image outward. The only thing visible to the rest of the world is the image being projected. The language of a codependent Projector involves taking what they really are on the inside and using it to describe someone else. If they are angry people then they will describe others as angry, if controlling then others have control problems, if egotistical then the rest of the world is full of pride. Projectors are codependents that are experts at avoidance. They are also characterized by a temperament of being overwhelmed and blaming others as the cause, when they actually create the stressful situations themselves.

Projectors are emotionally, mentally, and spiritually immature. They are the last to admit this condition or accept it, but are quite sure that other people have these problems. Some people who are already in recovery for addiction will develop this codependent issue. All addicts are codependents, but not all are ready to accept it. When the deeper issues related to codependency surface they will become Projectors using the success of the primary recovery as a method of avoidance. Instead of seeking recovery for the secondary issue of codependency the same as they did the primary one, they turn the lamp off and stay in the dark. However, if life causes a codependent disturbance then the switch turns on. Projectors continue to cause damage in personal relationships because their codependency keeps them locked in a cycle of denial and blaming others for their problems.

Other Projectors, who have a temperament of being overwhelmed, are usually the ones who set the stage ahead of time. One such example was a woman who played the "sugar bowl" game every day with her kids. She would place the sugar bowl up high in the cupboard where it was out of reach of the children. At breakfast time they would ask for the sugar and she would have a big emotional reaction by projecting the image of an overwhelmed mother who was already doing too much to be bothered. The problem was that after breakfast every morning she would put the sugar bowl back in the same place where it was too high for the children to reach, and then repeat the events day after day. The easiest thing to do would have been to put the sugar bowl in a new place where the children could reach it, but codependency would not allow her to do that. She needed something to blame, circumstances to point at, anything but look inside. It also blinded her to the emotional damage being done to the children.

Christian Projectors can blame the devil for things he has nothing to do with. Quite often this comes up relating to the thoughts people have in their own minds, saying how the devil must have given them the thought. While this is possible it is not always the case. Maybe some ownership is needed instead of projecting towards external evil. The scripture that refers to our thoughts in this manner says, "*We demolish arguments and every pretension that sets itself up against the knowledge of God, and we take captive every thought to make it obedient to Christ.*" II Corinthians 10:5.

Ron E. #2 is a man who has been a Christian most of his life. His upbringing was mildly codependent, not too dysfunctional but not void of the issues either. One day he told me that he could not seem to get rid of the discouraging and judging thoughts the devil kept putting in his mind. I suggested he stop blaming the devil and take ownership. We discussed that taking those thoughts captive and making them obedient to Christ was not possible as long as he was projecting them onto the devil. To "take captive" and "make it obedient" implies deliberate action on our part. We cannot take something captive and project it onto something else at the same time. Ron E. #2 agreed to try a different approach and claims the thoughts as his own; in other words, remain focused internally where change could occur. He later told me for the first time he was having success in not having those thoughts discourage him. It was a simple change, but had a profound impact. Instead of being codependent by focusing externally and looking for the solution outside of himself, he was being dependent on Christ and the Bible for truth and power, and it worked.

Codependent Projectors can also be people who want desperately to be in a permanent relationship. The problem is their codependent nature causes their internal issues to remain hidden, until they are brought out and projected onto the relationship. They will hide their true character in an attempt to be accepted, setting up the failure of the relationship right from the beginning. If someone points out their character problems, they will adamantly deny that any problem exist and argue endlessly. However, the problems will surface and they will have to project them onto the other person or leave the relationship altogether. Then, they can just turn off the images and are left with the pain of loneliness or the desire to get back into the relationship. Turning off the light in a projector does not remove the content of what was on the inside; it only hides it from the outside world. People who repeat bad relationships or go in and out of the same ones often have this problem. Instead of having loving dependent relationships they have dysfunctional codependent ones, and never see themselves as the cause. The only true hope for people with this form of codependency is to begin the process of cleaning up on the inside instead of projecting onto the outside. Jesus spoke of this condition when he said, "*On the outside you appear to people as righteous but on the inside you are full of hypocrisy and wickedness.*" Matthew 23:28. Projectors can do a lot of damage to themselves and others.

Many years ago I listened to a tape of a well-known recovery speaker by the name of Bob Earl, someone who was publicly open about his recovery. He was also a scriptwriter for an old television series called "Ironside." In the recorded message he talked about getting ready to go on vacation and having to hurry and write the script for one of the episodes, then quickly leave town. Upon arriving at the destination, the hotel clerk handed him a letter from the producer, telling him the script was the worst he had ever written. They demanded that he cancel his vacation and return home immediately. Bob said his wife asked just one question: "Are you going to open the envelope?" He was staring at the envelope and had projected the whole content of the letter without even opening it. When Bob read the letter he found out the producer was actually complimenting his work, congratulating him for some of the best he had ever done.

That is what codependent Projectors will do, thinking they have everything in focus only to find out it was blurred all along. If they are phony then other people are the phony ones. If someone points out his inappropriate behavior, then the person who called attention to it is inappropriate. When attention is focused on their obvious problems, they will project statements such as, "Oh yeah, well what about you?" Projectors are people who cannot handle criticism, so they have to reverse the roles and make it about the other person's faults. These are just a few examples of how circumstances further the development of the character problems. Without some type of recovery or healing the Projector can only do what they know how to do, project themselves outward.

A few other parallels to this analogy are that projectors can only play what has already been recorded. Codependent Projectors are typically repeating their past; they replay the "old tapes" over and over. It might be a bad movie but it's all they have. The risk of trying something new or facing their past is too difficult. It is easier to just do what is familiar. Another parallel is that recorded images are not real; they are only a reflection of something else. Projectors try to pre-determine the outcome before the events take place. They imagine how everything works out in the end, such as riding off into the sunset towards the good life. The problem is that people are not actors, life is not a movie, and the outcome is not scripted. This delusion sets people up for the reality of a bad outcome, the very thing they are attempting to avoid. Codependent Projectors are masters of illusion — externally focused in a constantly changing world, reversing the roles of responsibility, living in emotional, mental, and spiritual extremes.

It would be nice if people with this condition could just take an honest look at themselves and change. While this could represent a goal to strive for, it's too big of a leap for Projectors. People with this condition need to identify the obstacles that stand in the way of self-honesty, many of which are addressed in chapters three through five. Peeling back the layers instead of trying to slash to the core is a better approach.

The Prisoner

Just like circumstances can produce character defects, they can also produce tools for helping people. One such tool came out of helping a family who had an adult child with an addiction, specifically a husband and wife who decided to seek help through our recovery ministry. Their adult son had been abusing drugs for several years and was creating chaos in the home. They came to the support groups out of desperation, having tried everything they knew only to see the situation get worse.

I met with them at their home to see if there was any additional help that could be provided. Neither of them drank alcohol or used drugs; in fact, they came from a multi-generational Christian family. Their son was the first one with an addiction, but there was at least some presence of codependency in the family. They were afraid to leave their house, go on vacation, or anything else that would present opportunity for their son to use the home. If they locked him out he would just break in. During our conversation, I commented, *"They had become prisoners in their own home."*

This scenario plays out on a regular basis in various ways but has one common characteristic: loss of freedom by the family. The addict, who usually gets this stronghold because they have avoided consequences, has taken over and controls the situation. This is one of the greatest opportunities to understand that recovering from codependency is not a matter of controlling the external circumstances, which includes the addict. It is a matter of people focusing on their own codependency, and making changes in the areas they already have control over. Nothing can take this away from someone except his or her own codependency. *"We are not helpless victims of another person's addiction; we are prisoners of our own decisions."* It is equally true that nothing can change until this condition is recognized. Victims stay Prisoners that are controlled by external circumstances in a constantly changing world, living in reversed roles that are extreme in nature.

This couple began making changes. The challenge came when their son was arrested on drug charges and they did not want to rescue him, which turned out to be part of the problem since he had been arrested and rescued several times before. It was interesting to speak with them the day the arrest happened, when the mother called and said, "I know you taught us what to do, but actually doing it is so hard." When given the chance to repeat their mistakes they did not, and instead let their son reap what he had sown. Then, a plan was immediately made which included reserving a bed at a treatment program. On Monday they went to court, and told the judge their son could go to treatment or sit in jail but he was not coming home. This young man sat there in total shock, not exactly what he had expected based on previous experiences. He later said that was the moment he changed, and the next hours sitting in his cell were the longest of his life. He took the treatment option, and has since achieved years of being clean and sober, is working with other young men to overcome addiction, and serving as a leader in the recovery community. Just as important is the fact that his parents are no longer codependent Prisoners.

Not all circumstances turn out this way but one thing is for sure, it's not even possible as long as the addict makes everyone else prisoners to their addiction. The truth set this family free, the one about reaping and sowing. In Galatians chapter six it states, *"Do not be deceived: God cannot be mocked. A man reaps what he sows."* God cannot bless a situation that is actively violating His Word. Codependent Prisoners are set free when they realize that they are the ones keeping themselves locked up, and change.

Prisoners are also people who have trouble following the rules. They seem to be experts about how things are supposed to work, at least in their own eyes. Proverbs 14:12 and 16:25 say, "*there is a way that seems right to a man, but in the end it leads to death.*" Just as with other forms of codependency, there are varying degrees of how this applies. Some prisoners are in minimum security, and others are on death row. Some codependents stay Prisoners for their entire lives, others change and experience freedom. People who have become prisoners to someone else's addiction will have to experience the truth of their condition before making changes. A friend of mine who did some time in the county jail said it was full of innocent people, at least according to the inmates. Denying the truth never leads to freedom, especially for codependents.

Think about the idea of an "intervention." Whether you have firsthand experience, just tried to help someone, or watched a show on television, the basic concept is the same. People want to confront someone who has an addiction, but success is often based on preparing those who are attempting the intervention first. Why is this necessary? Why do the professionals on television shows intervene with the family first? Could it be that the codependent prisoners need to be set free before the addicted one can be approached? The answer is yes, because there is a way that seems right, but is not.

My personal experience of working with families is that they often feel helpless and believe that nothing can be done to change the circumstances. Not all families are ready for the truth, that they can make changes with or without the cooperation of the addict. Codependent Prisoners have a hard time hearing this, especially when we start talking about their contribution to the problem. To them it sounds like a sentence of "guilty" when they are convinced of their innocence. Just like the inmates in the county jail, no one is set free by denying the condition of their confinement. That is just a dream world full of denial. But sometimes the families are tired of being Prisoners and are ready to be honest. It takes a lot of courage to make that simple step, but it opens the doors to new possibilities.

How this plays out in real life is that the family sees their mistakes and stops enabling or rescuing. *"You cannot violate God's Word and receive a blessing."* When the process of reaping and sowing is interrupted by the family, then the roles are reversed and the family becomes the prisoners to the addiction. One mom told me that they thought their family was doing everything right, only to find out that most of it was wrong. A painful admission of truth, but it was the key to freedom. Sometimes this condition is based on obligation to family rules that were passed down through generations, ones that are codependent in nature and ineffective. Other times cultural rules keep people locked in a state of limited choices, or perhaps religious traditions exist that are not supposed to be questioned. Whatever the case, codependent prisoners need to know the truth about them because *"the truth will set you free."* John 8:32. Change in families dealing with problems often starts with one person accepting truth, and making changes.

The Missionary

The term missionary is typically used for people who move to a foreign country in their service to God. Missionaries can also be domestic and remain inside their native country. People can serve in inner-city missions where they've never lived before, or serve in a rural setting when they grew up in a large city. The common characteristic for those who are codependent Missionaries is that they move away from their problems to serve God, only to find their problems arrive at their destination.

Unable to form healthy relationships with people back home, they run off to save the world as a solution. Eventually these people will become just as dysfunctional in the mission field because they never really solved their problems, they just relocated them. There is really no difference between the codependent

Missionary and the addict who uses geographical changes to solve their problems. Both will find out the hard way that the reason nothing gets better is because they show up in the new location.

Missionary couples that leave their home in the United States to spread the Gospel in a foreign country are truly making a commitment in their service to God. Many will spend their entire lives serving God to help others. There are no perfect people — all missionaries are sinners — but those who have untreated codependency will follow a pattern. At first everything will be wonderful as they serve and build new opportunities. Then the inevitable will happen, one situation after another, where the inability to deal with people and problems will surface in their codependent natures. They will try to depend on a new location and eternal focus to solve their personal issues. It will work temporarily, but ultimately it will cause more harm than good as people from other countries become confused with the contradiction between the message and the messenger.

These situations are made even worse when the codependent missionary moves around within the same country or area. This points to the outcome of all codependents with this trait: a trail of wreckage left behind. What is surprising about these situations is when the person never sees the reality of what they are doing. Can you imagine when the very people you came to share God with are the ones that can see mustard on your face when you can't? How tragic it is when people who want to give their lives to God's service remain locked in a cycle of dysfunctional living. Codependency will always blind people to their own problems.

People with this form of codependency will also choose professions in caretaking roles. Domestic Missionaries will work at homeless shelters, food kitchens, or in health care roles. They have a desire to help people, who are probably part of their God-given personality and spiritual gifts, but instead of a having a healthy dependence on God they are codependent with their profession. Basically, *"people are codependent Missionaries when their mission becomes dysfunctional."* It is true that they brought the problem into their profession, just as it is true that the profession increases the severity of the problem.

One thing is certain about codependent Missionaries: they will burn out. People can take the extreme contradiction for while, some more than others, but this form of codependency will ultimately take a person past their limit. This is why people who are clergy, counselors, and treatment professionals will leave their profession to save themselves. Some just cannot take working with people anymore, others see their dreams of serving God shattered by disappointment, and still others are told by doctors they will not live long without change.

Another area codependent Missionaries show up is in recovery. The surprise is that most of them have "long-term" sobriety or time in a recovery program. Bob Earl, who was mentioned earlier, talked about two men that he knew in a recovery program. Both of these men had 10 years of recovery, but were the most miserable and wretched people he knew that regularly attended meetings. Always complaining and grumbling, nothing ever good enough or right, masters of criticism. With that amount of sobriety they should have been carrying a message of hope, but their status as codependent Missionaries turned their message into a mess. There are plenty more like them. I personally knew a guy who had 12 years clean and sober, worked in a treatment program helping people get well, and went home one day and threw his living room furniture onto the front yard over a disagreement with his wife. A mutual friend commented accurately that he had yet to face the issues beyond addiction, specifically his codependency. Wherever a person goes, there they are.

An untreated codependent will be dysfunctional wherever they show up, whether in a recovery group, church, work environment or foreign country. Codependent Missionaries are on a mission, to hide their problems behind a veil of sacrifice and service.

The Abuser

This codependent title crosses all lines. Whether gender, profession, nationality, or economic status, name it and a codependent Abuser is not far from it. Men and women alike fit this title, those from any country, any line of work, or anyone from the slum to the country club. Abuse comes in many forms, and while some cross the lines morally, ethically, or legally, many others do not but still cause damage to people. So how can such a vast application be refined down to a description that can be used for codependent examples? The answer is to use the classic picture of the "Knight in Shining Armor and the Damsel in Distress."

In this example, we have a woman who needs to be rescued and a man who is ready for the task. She cries out in distress, he rushes in to save the day, and off to the castle they go. Before long there is a problem, and their roles are no longer needed. She does not need to be rescued and he has nothing to do. The opportunity to form a lasting relationship does not exist because their roles were temporary. This is where the rescuer becomes the abuser. There were expectations that went along with the service of rescuing, a debt is owed. The unspoken expectations are respect, servitude, and gratitude. If these are not met, the codependent nature of the rescuer comes out as abuse. The expectation is really about dependency, because he needs her to depend on him so his role as a rescuer receives its proper respect. When that does not happen, there is a price to pay.

One outcome is that their roles need to be re-established; in fact they depend on it. A crisis is needed, which gives a valid reason to create one. Sometimes we call these people "crisis junkies," if a problem does not exist they can easily create one. Put this type of a person together with a rescuer and you have codependency from both sides. The rescuer is also good at capitalizing on normal everyday problems to continue their role. The sad truth is that this describes too many relationships and marriages. Temporary roles based on the way they met, which do not work to develop loving dependent relationships.

Rob E. #4 is a codependent Abuser. While this side of his character was never directly revealed, it was obvious based on other characteristics of his personality, actions, and choices. One day while riding my bike I came across a woman who was broke down on the highway and standing outside her vehicle. I stopped and asked if she needed help, and let her use my cell phone to call her boyfriend. She said she was on her way to work and needed to get there. She was also alone on the side of the highway so I waited for her boyfriend to arrive before continuing my ride.

While we waited she was very complimentary of her new boyfriend and how much better he was than the abusive relationship she just left. Sounded like a red flag to me, but it was not until Rob E. #4 arrived I saw the real picture. He jumped out of his car, ran up to where we were, stretched out his arms up in the air, and proclaimed, "I GOT IT." Not "Thank you," or "Are you OK?" to his girlfriend, nothing of that nature. There was just one other quick comment directed at me with a dead stare, "You can go now." I nodded and rode away on my bike. What was completely obvious was that Rob E. #4 was a rescuer who was fulfilling his role and was aggressive in making sure he was the only one. His body language, words, and actions clearly stated that he alone was the rescuer of this woman, and given all the warning signs would most likely be the next abuser in her life at some point in the future. His codependency was based on an unhealthy dependence, clearly from the role he played when they met, one that is far from what God established for loving dependent relationships.

Female rescuers can also be Abusers. Codependent women will attach themselves to needy men who need rescuing, especially if they have children. The same characteristics of the rescuing man applies to the woman as well, there is an expectation attached to the rescue, one of respect, servitude, and gratitude. When these expectations are not met, the Abuser comes out. People need to beware of this type of character, those who are eager to rescue might be nice people, clean, sober, churchgoer, and have good jobs, but their codependency is dangerous. Single parents are a target for this type of codependent. This is another codependent trait that most likely will require professional help to overcome.

Recovery can break the cycle of this type of codependency by helping people remove the need to be rescued, or the need to rescue others. The difficulty comes in knowing if a person is truly genuine in wanting to form a healthy relationship. Single parents have more than just their own security to think about. This world is full of good examples of people who raised or influenced children who were not their own biologically. Even Jesus was raised by his stepfather Joseph. But it is as true that there are codependent Abusers disguised as good people who commonly engage in rescuing. The hard truth is the best protection against this type of person is to be healthy yourself. Healthy people attract healthy people, dysfunctional people attract dysfunctional people, and codependent people attract needy people. The tendency to repeat bad relationships is greater for those who do not heal from their past than those who do. *"Personal healing is the best protection against a codependent Abuser."*

The Public Defender

Codependents are quite often driven by the need to defend other people, causes, or organizations. The focus is on anything external that provides an opportunity to voice an opinion, plead a case, or influence an outcome. The difference between a real public defender and a codependent one is that while real ones are court-appointed, codependent ones appoint themselves.

People by nature like to be connected with other people. Civic or service organizations are productive ways for people to join together and work for the community. Healthy servants in these organizations have an honest motive to give, the same as churches or recovery programs who help others. But the codependent Public Defender needs something; they need to win. Their external validation requires it, and their participation in groups is really about taking and not giving. Sure, they will talk like a giving person, until something doesn't go their way. Codependents with this trait will expose themselves when problems arise, because anytime there's a winner, there's also a loser.

There is actually a wide range of ways this type of codependent expresses themselves. One is to threaten to write a letter when a situation goes awry. They like to say, "I'm going to write a letter" to some person or company, as if it represents a real threat of influence. The idea is that someone needs to defend the cause and they are just the person to do it. What this is really about is fantasy, because it is all in their own head. They will imagine great public recognition for their thoughts being respected and shared with others. In the past a codependent Public Defenders probably would not get their letters published even if they did actually write one, but social media has changed all that. The ability to easily publish an opinion on a public level has given many codependents exactly what they needed, unlimited access to the external world. When several Public Defenders get started on a string of social media comments, it can become quite a spectacle of ignorance. Read the comment threads and you will find a lot of dysfunctional codependents defending their cause or opinion, but you will have to search for a while to locate any true wisdom.

Another expression of the codependent Public Defender is being offended, which ties closely to the letter writer but takes a different direction. Being offended by what is wrong is a characteristic that God possesses. He is offended by sin, and by things people do that contradict His laws and His ways of living (more about being offended as it relates to codependency will be covered in chapter five). Role reversal takes God's way of living and makes it seem bad, which opens the door for people to decide for themselves what is right and wrong. Codependent Public Defenders are easily offended, thus giving them a reason to appoint themselves as defenders of "the cause" and redefine right from wrong. While this certainly applies to politics, what about our own homes and personal relationships?

Conflict is a given in families, it is not a matter of "if" it will happen, only a matter of "when." The Public Defender who is regularly offended will carry the same role into close personal relationships. This is also where the difference between a real public defender and a codependent one exist; a self-appointed one makes themselves the judge and jury as well. No one can be allowed to win except the codependent. Disagreements with this type of person are rarely mild because they quickly turn into arguments and extreme expressions of emotion. In their minds they have already pictured themselves in a court of law pleading their case and always winning. It becomes like an old movie, playing over and over and over. But when they have to exit this fantasy world and attempt to form loving dependent relationships, they cannot. Instead they argue, plead their case, and sit in judgment of everyone else.

Rose E. #10 is a woman I met through our church who was very codependent but refused to use any recovery tools, since in her opinion they were obviously bad. She had a tendency to always be late no matter what the occasion. She shared with me one of the methods she was using to solve the problem, setting her own clock ahead of the real time, which was really comical. I always wondered how that was going to work when the person moving the clock ahead is the same one using it to be on time. Anyway, she was still always late. So her husband, who did not like to be late, attempted to address the issue. The result was an argument about how it was everyone else's fault that she was always late. A bit strange considering that she had adjusted her clock to solve a problem that in her opinion was everyone else's fault. But that was not all. The husband told me that the next time they got ready to leave for church he looked around the house for Rose E. #10 and could not find her. She had not said a word to anyone, but left the house and was sitting in the car out in the driveway, just to prove that she was not the cause of being late. She had to win. This public defense of her character defects was not a solution to her problems or a way to build loving dependent relationships. Codependency is called dysfunctional for a reason.

Another expression is from people who cannot properly handle criticism without defending themselves. This ties to the all-or-nothing extremes; it is either fight or flight when it comes to Public Defenders handling criticism. The balance that we need personally is to listen to criticism and decide if it's valid or not. We can choose to accept or reject criticism, but trying to explain or defend it is an expression of codependency. This is where a perfectionist has trouble because they cannot allow themselves to make mistakes. God allows us to be human, but a perfectionist will make up their own rules where mistakes are not allowed by themselves or others. They cannot handle criticism, so they must put up a solid defense. Any risk of being publicly exposed of having made a mistake must be avoided at all cost. The codependent Public Defender tries to survive in a world without criticism, which is pure delusion.

The Skunk

These animals are well known for the way they defend themselves. A skunk will make its way through life relatively undetected until it is threatened. At that point it will use its own self-defense to repel enemies by spraying them with a stinky substance, one that is already inside of them and readily available at all times.

The codependent Skunk will have one of the same characteristics of all codependents, internal issues that are being hidden. The difference is when this person feels threatened, either real or perceived, they will spray you with their issues in a way that repels. The goal is to run other people off as a self-defense mechanism.

I have met more codependent Skunks than I would care to admit. They are not the ones who are attending recovery groups, involved in any kind of counseling, or getting help of any kind for their codependent issues. They roam about undetected, hiding their best defense weapon against the external world. Unfortunately, the way you find out who they are is when a problem arises that threatens their security, and they spray you. It can come through their words or actions, but once you have been sprayed by a Skunk, it just stays with you for a while. These types of people are toxic with their codependency.

This codependent will also be very territorial in their area of influence. They will be on guard for any intruders that try to get into their area. Anyone can be a threat. A real skunk perceives any intrusion as a threat, codependent Skunks do the same. The other similarity is the smell of a skunk stays with you if you get sprayed; in fact it is very difficult to get rid of. The effectiveness of a codependent Skunk is based on their ability to spray you with something that will stay with you when you leave. Their comments are aggressive, and their actions are deliberate. The important thing is that you are repelled, continue to experience the stench, and stay away.

One of the names given to some church members who have been around for a long time is the "old guard." The picture is that of a person who has influence and control over certain areas that they continue to guard against intruders. All long-term church members do not fit this description, but it can happen even to good people over time. The risk is if someone remains in the ranks of the "old guard" too long they will become a Skunk. The circumstances will cause the progression of their codependent issues; they will forget that Jesus Christ is the head of the church. The problem centers on the fact that any function of the church is an opportunity for new people to get involved. Anything from music to maintenance can be someone's personal ministry, unless they are a Skunk. Then they will spray anyone who gets too close and poses a threat, real or perceived.

I have heard of circumstances where new church members wanted to help in the office or grounds keeping and walked away with the message that they had invaded someone's space. Other situations involved the music ministry, where someone new wanted to sing or help with sound equipment and got repelled. One codependent Skunk would actually tell people straight out that if they touched the soundboard there would be trouble. This could be understood if someone was adjusting equipment they had no business touching, but not when the person wants to help or learn and is deliberately run off. One older gentleman told me that he offered to help the volunteer maintenance man with a project at church, but left with the certain message that he was not welcome and had crossed the line into another man's territory.

It is important to understand that these examples represent the minority and not the majority. There are far more examples of good people using their personal area of service in the church as an outreach to others. They welcome new people with enthusiasm and genuine care. Yet there are also examples that are hard to understand, of how someone could act the way they act and speak the way they speak, unless you apply the analogy of the skunk. Then it makes sense — it looks great if you keep your distance, but getting too close will get you sprayed. It might make you wonder what that person is really like on the inside, but it is another example of what Jesus was talking about when he said, "*You are like whitewashed tombs, which look beautiful on the outside but on the inside are full of the bones of the dead and everything unclean. In the same way, on the outside you appear to people as righteous but on the inside you are full of hypocrisy and wickedness.*" Matt. 23:27.

The good news is that recovery from codependency cleans up the inside. People who have this personality trait can eventually learn to work with others and use their service in productive ways if they can be honest and change.

The Master Chef

Codependents live in a world of fantasy. The control they believe they have over people and circumstances is not real. Psalm 51:6 can help to solve this problem, which states that God *"desires truth in the inward parts"* of who we are. The way some codependents avoid this exercise is to become a Chef, which requires taking an ounce of truth, combining it with a pound of lies, and cooking up something deceitful to serve others. The only thing a codependent Chef needs is people who are a little hungry for some dysfunctional cuisine. After a while and with lots of practice they will graduate to the level of Master Chef, the very best at what they do.

People who like to gossip are codependent Chefs. The proof is in the fact that gossips depend on other people to listen. The only thing they need is other people who are hungry for some tasty lies. If a Chef prepares a meal and no one is around to enjoy it, they will deliver. The whole problem exists in the fact that what they are serving to others only has a small element of truth. The rest is there to make it appealing so others will accept it.

This characteristic is actually part of our healthy dependence on God, but codependency will ruin it and send it in the wrong direction. We learn this from a request made to Jesus by His closest followers: *"The apostles said to the Lord, 'Increase our faith!' He replied, 'If you have faith as small as a mustard seed, you can say to this mulberry tree, 'Be uprooted and planted in the sea, and it will obey you.'"* Luke 17:5-6. The Lord was teaching us that our contribution to living by His will is actually a small part of the big picture; the rest will be supplied by Him. The apostles wanted more faith, and Jesus told them to focus on having a small amount. Would the tree be uprooted because their words were powerful? No, it would happen because they understood when a small amount of faith is combined with a lot of dependence on God that great things will happen. Codependency will replace dependence on God with dependence on self, and the gap between our small contribution and the remaining void will be filled by us. A divine influence will be replaced with a sinful one; truth will be substituted with lies. This is the problem of the codependent Chef. They can take a mustard seed's worth of truth and combine it with their own agenda, which consists of fear, resentment, manipulation, pain, and many other hurtful issues. What they create has to be shared with others.

I heard a speaker say that "gossiping is talking about a person when you are not part of the problem or the solution." This is a good gauge to measure someone's motives. One of the questions I have used when talking with a person that starts gossiping about someone else is to ask them if it is okay for me to share the information with the person they are talking about. A person that is part of the solution should not have a problem with this request. A codependent Chef will quickly decline. Their role in gossiping is to keep the story going; they depend on it to continue. Honesty and solutions would otherwise end the conversation.

The real destructive nature of this issue is when a codependent Master Chef destroys the name or reputation of another person. Those who are unable to form healthy relationships will acquire this trait to give themselves a reason to divorce a marriage, leave a job, or just run away. There are similarities here with the codependent Projector that needs relationships but cannot maintain them. Master Chefs are just different in how they create the exit plan: by taking a small amount of truth, combining it with a lot of lies, and cooking up something that will provide a reason to leave. It seems that in the case of marriages the reason given quite often is "abuse." After all, who could fault a person for saving themselves from an abusive relationship? But what if that person is a codependent Master Chef who is cooking up lies about the abuse?

I have listened to this scenario many, many, many times, conversations with genuinely good people who are being slandered by a spouse who wants a divorce. These people are having the truth — that they raised their voice, said something mean, or got angry — used as an excuse to label them as abusive. Verbal abuse is never acceptable, but neither is distorting the truth by lying. These situations involve people who through their own codependency are unable to form loving dependent relationships, and instead of looking inside where the real problems are, they have to focus externally and reverse the roles. When I have talked with the person who is being lied about, it is obvious they are the ones who are being abused, by the Chef. What makes this worse is when a Master Chef is cooking up the lies, because they are really good at what they do from years of experience. They can make a good person look like a really bad one, and convince other people that it's all true. At the same time they can take their bad character and make it look good. Master Chefs are really good at playing the victim role.

If a person is honestly in an abusive relationship, they typically do not run around gossiping to everyone else about it. The sad truth is that people who are being abused often hide the problem, have trouble getting out of the relationship, or will actually go back to an abusive relationship once they get out. While these challenges may have their own issues, they are not the same as what is being discussed here. The person running around spreading lies with the sole purpose of tearing other people down is different. They are the abuser, and comparing themselves to people are truly being abused is emotionally, mentally, and spiritually sick.

One note about the true victim of the codependent Chef: the person who is being slandered. They typically have their own codependent issues that need recovery, counseling, or some type of healing. It is just a different kind of codependency, but if someone has been in a dependent relationship with a person capable of being a Chef, they will have their own codependent issues to resolve. Otherwise they are doing the same thing by blaming the other person as the source of all the problems. Setting boundaries with the lies of the other person while taking an honest look at their own issues will go a long way towards healing.

The Anaconda

Just the word can bring about images of fear and the desire to avoid any contact with this creature. Real anacondas move gracefully, undetected, then ever so gently wrap around their victim before literally putting the squeeze on. Then it slowly applies force to take the life out of whatever is inside of its grip.

A codependent Anaconda can be a nice person, caring, loving, and kind. The main goal of this type of codependent is to not be detected, never viewed as a person who can cause great harm. They have to get close to people first, which requires a high level of dishonesty in relationships. They are best known by the trail of wreckage left in their past, which needs to be hidden from the new opportunity so the threat is not recognized. An Anaconda cannot let the truth get out, so they act in a manner that raises no suspicions.

Public examples of this type of person will occasionally make it to the media. A person who marries someone from another country thinking they really know the person, only to find out there was a lot hidden from them. When the truth comes out it can be too late; the victim now has the Anaconda wrapped around them and cannot escape. Sometimes it is women who marry a man then travel to his country of origin thinking everything is wonderful, only to find themselves trapped in a subservient role with no way out. Men and women alike can be this type of codependent.

The more common examples are people who have a history of failed relationships, but need to keep the details hidden from a new prospect. They are usually practicing some form of self-denial as well, refusing to believe that they are the problem. These people will carefully get close to another person without raising any suspicion they pose a threat. Then after they have wrapped their lives around the other person's, they will gradually start to squeeze. The victim of the codependent Anaconda will at some point realize the person they decided to form a relationship with is not the same person they are with currently. They might wonder how they missed this side of the person, but by that time it is too late and trying to escape is not so easy. Their lives are now firmly in the grip of the threat.

It is naïve to think that a Christian could never be this type of person, but as with many objections the real life testimonies prove otherwise. Rose E. #6 was such a person. She had been going to church since a youth, always active in helping out, and a flaming codependent. After multiple failed marriages she met the man of her dreams, and they married. Several months into the marriage the husband spoke with me about the chaos in the home. He said that he could not believe the extreme nature of her character, the fits of anger, inability to deal with problems, and constant arguing over every little detail of life. He said that one day he even got scolded for leaving breadcrumbs on the butter; he could do nothing right in her eyes. He went on to explain that he tried to talk with her about the problems, asking where all this came from because he never saw it before they got married. Her response was devastating; she told him, "I hid it from you." Rose E. #6 was a codependent Anaconda, who moved in gradually and carefully to avoid detection, but eventually wrapped herself around another victim and proceeded to squeeze the life out of him. A few years later the result was death to the marriage, another divorce.

The basic elements of this example will play themselves out in a variety of circumstances. People get hired into jobs only to find out an employer fooled them. Some enter into business with a person they think they know well, only to find out later their business partner is an unethical or immoral person who has a trail of problems from their past. Still others naively put faith and trust in another person just because they are both Christians, as if it must be good because it could never be bad. Then after the train wreck they find out it was not the first time the other person deceived someone. The character of the codependent Anaconda is solely based on two things: deception and taking. They are masters at role reversal, making themselves look good when in fact they are not.

Just as common as the pattern of the codependent Anaconda is the fact that their victims are also codependent, just in another form. People are deceived because they are not depending on the truth. These are the ones who will avoid any type of premarital counseling, because if the truth were known they might have to make the tough decision to end the relationship. Think of the insanity of avoiding the truth about the person you want to marry just so you can stay together, only to find out the truth about them after you are married. Codependency seems to take away the ability of certain people to use good judgment.

The Victim

When it comes to the subject of victims there are two categories: true victims and false ones. True victims are not codependents, but false ones are. All of the basic elements of codependency come to bear on this characteristic: role reversal by taking what is false and making it look true, living externally focused in a constantly changing world, and living in the extremes emotionally, mentally, and spiritually. Codependent Victims depend on the external problems of this world to avoid looking inside themselves. They are skilled at becoming victims of circumstances that have nothing to do with them, or attaching to a cause that gives reason for extreme emotional expressions.

Even though from Ecc. 1:3 we know that *"there is nothing new under the sun,"* we also know some cultural issues come and go through time. History has taught us there are times when these problems go away only to resurface in another time and culture. Through this we can understand some things are common to mankind. They have always been in the world and always will be, not as a constant but more in highs and lows. Such is the case with codependent Victims.

The book of Genesis records the first victims in the story of creation. After sin entered the garden, God had a question and answer session with the culprits. Adam tried to play the role of victim by blaming Eve, and Eve picked up very quickly on that game and blamed the serpent. God knew what they were up to and put an end to the role reversal game. He never asked the serpent why. He just started handing out consequences in the reverse order of the questioning. They all chose not to follow God's rules and made up their own, to set their own scales of balance, and it failed because they chose to depend on themselves instead of God.

Our world today is at another peak of false victims masquerading as real ones. Perhaps we see it more because of the use of media to quickly share information, but this could actually be more of the cause than a symptom. People who are codependent need something to depend on, and they often need others to depend on it with them. Mainstream and social media provide ample opportunity for codependent Victims to find something to attach to. The trend of the victimization of America is nothing new, and neither is its connection to codependency.

It would be easy to say that false victims are only hurting themselves, just as people used to say about alcoholism. But we know that alcoholics and drug addicts hurt more than just themselves, and the same is true of codependents. False victims take it a step further and claim they are not actually hurting anyone, believing they are helping to bring out truth and justice. That is a lie because codependent Victims are looking for something, they need something, and they are not going to stop until they get it. They do not care who has to lose so they can win, or who will suffer for their selfishness. What matters to false victims is reversing the roles and being recognized as a true victim.

In families, codependent Victims will also play the martyr role. A common expression that some have coined the $10,000 codependent statement is "Look at all that I do for you and this is the thanks I get." The message is the person who is helping is being victimized by the ungrateful recipients of their help. Never mind the other people did not want or ask for help, they are not grateful for getting it. This could come with something as simple as household chores or financial assistance, but no matter what the subject, it is selfish in nature. God's way of helping people is to do so without expectation.

Our example is Christ, who was a true victim but never claimed to be one. In fact, He taught us what our motive should be in helping others when He said, *"The Son of Man did not come to be served, but to serve, and to give his life as a ransom for many."* Matthew 20:28. Could you imagine if Jesus had said, "Look at all that I'm doing for you, and this is the thanks I get"? He certainly would not be the Savior if He had. We are directed multiple times in Scripture to model our lives after Christ. If anyone had the right to be a victim it was Jesus, but He forgave and prayed for his abusers. Codependent Victims will default to their "rights" when threatened or perceive to be threatened. They will never break free of the bondage of being a victim until they embrace the principles given by Jesus.

The Environmentalist

This codependent title is the most controversial of them all. While it would be nice to avoid any political hot topics, there are just too many connections between environmentalism and codependency to leave it out. There is so much emotion invested in being a true "environmentalist" that those who claim it often become hypersensitive, especially to anything or anyone that does not agree. They rarely have just one codependent title; more often than not they possess multiple titles that are used to express their concerns or opposition. It also seems that those who prefer being environmentalists do not see its connection to codependency. Every principle common to codependency applies to this title.

With terms that are being used in more recent history such as global warming, climate change, urban sprawl, tree huggers, animal rights advocate, and so on, one would think this is a new topic. However, the subject is actually rooted in the commandments God made in the Garden of Eden. He told man to rule over the earth and subdue it. It is within human nature to take care of the earth because we were commanded to do so by its Creator. Those who abuse it have to violate their own conscience to do so, whether they realize it or not. A person who makes selfish decisions towards abusing creation and then says they do not care is someone who has simply become deaf to their own conscience. Also, the creation story covers all animals and plants, which is why environmentalism includes both topics. It should be no surprise that people who are tree huggers tend to be the same who advocate animal rights. We are not as unique and independent as we think; some things were established long before we were born and are common to mankind.

We can understand our connection to the environment from the book of Genesis Chapter 1:27-29: "*So God created mankind in his own image, in the image of God he created them; male and female he created them. God blessed them and said to them, Be fruitful and increase in number; fill the earth and subdue it. Rule over the fish in the sea and the birds in the sky and over every living creature that moves on the ground.*" Then God said, "*I give you every seed-bearing plant on the face of the whole earth and every tree that has fruit with seed in it. They will be yours for food.*" We also have to keep in mind a familiar scripture to the topic of codependency: "*There is nothing new under the sun.*" Ecclesiastes 1:3.

God created the earth and gave mankind the responsibility to take care of it. Keeping in mind that "*codependency occurs anytime dependence exceeds the limits that God has established,*" we can begin to see how environmentalism takes a God-given principle to a dysfunctional extreme and reverses the roles from Godly dependence to human dependence. When people take their responsibility to care for the earth beyond what God established, then they are playing God in the world around them, asserting influence and control over things that were never intended to be under their control. God as the Creator will control the outcome of His creation; codependency assumes that He needs help to get it right. An appropriate question was asked centuries ago: "*Why do the nations conspire and the peoples plot in vain?... The One enthroned in heaven laughs; the Lord scoffs at them.*" Psalm 2:1, 4. Environmentalism is nothing more than an expression of codependency that attempts to take God out of the role of being responsible for creation.

There are times when violations of God's standards help to push truth to the surface. Such is the case with codependent Environmentalism. In order for a relationship to become a loving dependent one, there needs to be genuine intimacy. A one-sided relationship is codependent; a loving dependent relationship requires giving and receiving from both sides. When these are kept in proper balance we can experience true intimacy. Some people think that the highest expression of intimacy is sex, but that is not true. Just being able to perform the physical act does not produce intimacy. As with all relationships, God is our standard. Our relationship with Him is a loving dependent relationship. It is based on giving and receiving, with both sides reciprocating love to each other. God loves us, and wants us to love Him. We experience the highest form of intimacy when we love God and receive His unconditional love for us. Those who have personally experienced God's love know the difference.

"*Environmentalism is a one sided relationship without intimacy.*" The emotions are created by only one side, the codependent Environmentalist, which cannot be reciprocated by a plant, tree, rock, mountain, or even the planet. The environment also cannot reciprocate emotions by expressing gratitude. A person has to manufacture this for themselves through being convinced of all the wonderful things they are doing, when really they are just playing God by thinking that they have control over the destiny of the world. It is an extreme form of codependency. Eventually environmentalists will expose their other trait, a codependent Translator, by using the familiar statement "Oh, so you're saying that (insert opposite extreme)." If you try to oppose their agenda, they will try to say you don't care about the earth at all. It is very hard for a codependent Environmentalist to truly understand healthy dependence.

The subject of animals is one side of this type of codependency that really confuses people. Animals have characteristics that are closer to human than plants or trees. It is very easy for codependents to get confused about animals, to take God's established principles to an extreme. The way this is accomplished is to gradually put animals and humans on the same level, and since enough is never enough, eventually elevate animals above humans. This has been happening in our modern world, where the abuse of animals by people has lead to the opposite extremes where animals are not just protected, but elevated above human beings. The codependent Environmentalist is proud of this achievement, but since it violates God's standard it can only lead to dysfunctional results. It is also a repeated pattern of history. Abusing animals is never acceptable, but neither is the extreme of protecting them to the point of elevating their value above humans.

History is full of cultures that gradually elevated animals above human beings. Some have combined humans with animals to create mythical characters. There are examples where people have determined that dogs guard the gates of heaven, certain types of animals are deity, or past ancestors are reincarnated as animals. The examples are endless and timeless. Yet all of them have one thing in common, a departure from the standards established in the Bible. In order to elevate animals as being equal or above humans, you have to violate God's Word. We were told to care for the animals, not to determine their order of importance in creation. Codependent Environmentalists will have an even harder time with animals than trees because they feel that an animal's affection is reciprocating intimacy in a relationship. Kept in proper balance we can experience, love, and enjoy our pets, but remove God's standards from the picture and people will go to extremes. They will claim that a mutual affection exist, one that can be defined as intimacy, which is why we now see people wanting to marry their pets. They are confused about creation because they are making up their own standards based on feelings and not on truth.

The proper balance between humans and animals was established in Genesis as well. Just after creation was completed we have the story of the first sin, the "fall of man." God's response to sin at the end of Genesis Chapter 3 provides a clear picture of the order of priority, when God killed an animal to provide clothes for Adam and Eve. He could have used trees or plants, the same as they did by using fig leaves. Instead, God corrects their error by sacrificing an animal. This principle continues through the Old Testament with the subject of animal sacrifices in the Temple for the atonement of sins. Eventually in the New Testament era Jesus came as the "Lamb of God" and was sacrificed for our sins. God has always held humans as a higher form of creation than animals or plants. Think about the fact that not only did the God of heaven come to earth in human form as the man Jesus Christ, but also placed himself below man to be killed like an animal, a sacrificial lamb, for the benefit of people. This is not some warm and fuzzy subject for people to get confused about regarding their pets; it is an important principle to help us keep the proper balance in the world, because *"codependency occurs anytime dependence exceeds the limits that God has established."*

A solid picture of the difference can be taken from the Old Testament sacrifices made in the tabernacle. Moses followed God's instructions to great detail in the offering of sacrifices. One example in Leviticus is enough to make the point.

"He then presented the ram for the burnt offering, and Aaron and his sons laid their hands on its head. Then Moses slaughtered the ram and splashed the blood against the sides of the altar. He cut

the ram into pieces and burned the head, the pieces and the fat. He washed the internal organs and the legs with water and burned the whole ram on the altar. It was a burnt offering, a pleasing aroma, a food offering presented to the Lord, as the Lord commanded Moses." Leviticus 18:18-21.

If people and animals are on the same level, then it would be acceptable to substitute a child for a ram and follow the same directions that were given to Moses. Try to imagine following these instructions in Leviticus 18 with a human child, and it won't take long for your own conscience to reject the idea with disgust. No one in his or her right mind could say that God would accept this as pleasing. There is a difference in the priority of creation between people and all other plants and animals, as established by the Creator. Our own conscience tells us so, unless it is overridden by a problem called codependency. Trying to take the high ground by saying it is not acceptable for animals either, is the same as stating that God is wrong and gave bad directions to Moses. When our personal beliefs collide with God's established principles, then we need to change, not Him.

Jesus spoke about this when He used the topics of plants and animals to reinforce mankind's value in God's eyes. *"Look at the birds of the air; they do not sow or reap or store away in barns, and yet your heavenly Father feeds them. Are you not much more valuable than they? ...See how the flowers of the field grow. They do not labor or spin. Yet I tell you that not even Solomon in all his splendor was dressed like one of these. If that is how God clothes the grass of the field, which is here today and tomorrow is thrown into the fire, will he not much more clothe you."* Matthew 6:26, 28-30. Jesus could have chosen any example to explain how valuable we are to God, but He specifically used plants and animals for the illustration. In doing so, He reminded us of the standard that was established in the Garden of Eden.

We can also apply the words God gave to Noah after the flood, another point of re-establishing the order of priority.

"The fear and dread of you will fall on all the beasts of the earth, and on all the birds in the sky, on every creature that moves along the ground, and on all the fish in the sea; they are given into your hands. Everything that lives and moves about will be food for you. Just as I gave you the green plants, I now give you everything." Genesis 9:2-3.

It is no wonder that so many codependent Environmentalists are vegetarians. Once a person departs from God's principles, they continue struggling to understand healthy dependence and proper balance. They will never understand how a person can care for animals and eat meat, but God understands, and so do people who accept his principles for living. Not all vegetarians are environmentalist, but many codependents Environmentalist are vegetarians.

Animals are guided by instinct that is their highest form of existence. People are also guided by instinct, but we have a soul that is a higher form of existence. When people live solely by their instincts they begin to act like animals, their choices and behavior seem to lack human conscience. The confusion comes when people assign conscience to animals and give them something God never gave them. They express their codependency as Environmentalist, externally focused, reversing the roles of what God established, living in the extremes of all or nothing. If you do not agree with their elevation of animals then they claim you don't care about animals. The truth is we can love and care for our pets, be respectful of those in the wild, and still understand we are above them in God's order of creation.

Correcting the problem of codependent Environmentalism is simple, but very difficult for those who are committed to their cause. As humans we depend on God to complete every area of our life, because we are limited. Without God we will go to extremes because spiritually we are incomplete and need the presence of the Holy Spirit. Ultimately we will all depend on God after our death. Who can determine their destiny after their body is dead? Only those who have depended on God's truth and accepted Christ as their Savior can have confidence in eternity. People who make up their own destiny by ignoring God's standards will feel good for now, confident in their decisions and ability to reason. But their dependence on self-generated truth will fail in the presence of God. The answer for the codependent Environmentalist is to admit that God is right, they are wrong, and accept the order of creation that was established by the Creator. Abuse of creation is not permission for people to go to the opposite extreme and exalt themselves in an effort to control the outcome, no matter how famous, high up in government, or emotionally-charged they are. Denying this does not remove the reality, it only creates the extremes. Those who want to save creation should consider one thing; "*What good will it be for someone to gain the whole world, yet forfeit their soul?*" Matthew 16:26.

There are certainly more titles that could be used in addition to the 24 given here. Codependency has many faces, but these provide quite a few descriptions for practical use. The main point is to identify with a description or analogy that makes it easy to realize when the codependency is coming to the surface and the tendency to use old habits is strong. The emotional and spiritual nature of codependency, along with the mental strain of old patterns, will make it difficult to change. And, as stated at the beginning, if these titles help you to better understand someone else, then use that information for self-improvement. The easier we can recognize someone else's tendencies, the better we can refrain from reacting and learn to respond. What often blocks us from that goal are the internal issues that we need to lose.

Are you ready to experience some abandonment?

3

Abandonment is the Central Theme
of Codependency

A *bandonment has to take place before codependency can* *exist.* Right dependence upon God and other people is void of abandonment. Under these conditions people can maintain the right standards within the limits God established and bad solutions will be rejected in favor of good decisions. This type of healthy dependence has to be abandoned before codependency can rise to the surface. It can happen at different degrees for a variety of subjects within the same person. We can make good choices in one area of our lives, while making bad decisions in another.

The subject of abandonment ties directly to codependency in the sense that a person has to abandon what is right and accept what is wrong to become codependent. For example, God's purpose for each person's life directly ties to their spiritual gifts. It is His will for these to be strengths and not weaknesses. When the characteristics of codependency are absent a person can express their gifts in a healthy and functional manner, otherwise they are expressed in a dysfunctional or codependent manner.

America itself is an example of this principle. Codependency has been around since the beginning of man, yet as dependence upon God has been gradually abandoned in America, codependency has risen to the surface. The less we depended on God the more we depended on ourselves and others, and ultimately depended on the government to meet our needs. It is my opinion there has been an increasing level of codependency in America, especially in the last 50 to 60 years; thus, people wonder why the culture has become so dysfunctional. It is not that America decades ago was a perfect place or a superior culture, but it was more dependent on God and was a society more in balance with the will of God.

Another example is men have become unemotional, resulting in cultural damage to the father-son relationship. This lack of emotional nurturing teaches boys that the strong silent type who never cries is a real man. What is good has become bad and what is bad has become good. If a man expresses painful emotions he is considered weak, while others go too far and become over-emotional with rage. Neither of these are true to God's plan for creation. Jesus was more of a man than any human father, yet He wept. He also loved, spoke truth when it was not convenient, and went out his way to help others. He sacrificed His life for all people including those who did not agree with what He was doing. He was a man's man, and placed dependence on the relationship with his Father above all things. Those who follow Jesus' example will have a loving dependent relationship with their Father in Heaven, which will affect their relationships on earth. Those who trade the truth for a lie will live in unbalanced extremes, abandoning the very dependence they need to face life's challenges. Christians are not void of this truth; a codependent Christian will lead a dysfunctional life.

Even with all this cultural confusion we can still face the subjects of abandonment and codependency on an individual level. God is looking for a heart that will trust in Him and depend on His divine wisdom and strength. The irony is that we have to abandon our self to experience God. What often stands in the way is codependency and addiction. Underneath these two issues lies an abundance of common human problems like pride, self-pity, bitterness, fear, lust, and so on. Some people will change their lives for a good enough reason; others will change to solve problems which have become more severe. But the person who has become codependent will have every reason to change, and will remain the same. They will hold on to the very things they need to let go of, and abandon any possibility of the peaceful life they so desperately desire. When this person finally chooses to change by abandoning their own best thinking and intentions, choosing to trust in God and other people, then they will move beyond codependency. It is an individual choice, and does not depend on the cooperation or support of others who are not ready to change.

To really get at the root of this issue and how it ties to codependency, we will need to look at three ways we experience abandonment: from others, ourselves, and God. All people experience these three expressions of abandonment, but not all are affected the same way. The difference is defined by our actions, in how these are currently being expressed in our lives. They can change over time by getting better or worse. It depends on what level of truth we are ready for. Peeling back the layers of the onion prepares us to look at deeper issues that we may not have been ready for in the past. Regardless of where we are, an honest look at these three areas of abandonment will aid in the process of overcoming codependency.

Abandoned by Others

This form of abandonment can take place physically, but also emotionally, mentally, and spiritually. It is possible to be physically present while emotionally unavailable, which is a common form of male codependency. A man who attended a family class said that his father was always around but he was never there. There was never any communication or connection. It was no surprise that he struggled to have loving dependent relationships, and his life was characterized by repeated failed attempts to form intimate bonds with other people.

Girls will also be affected by fathers that are present but absent. Reflecting on the principle from chapter one about the greatest influence in our lives, the strongest relationship in a young girl's life is between her father and herself. What is she going to do with an unemotional false example? It will create issues of abandonment that will result in dependency problems.

One night I was walking back to our house with my sons, who were between 10-14 years old at the time. We had gone to the local convenience store to get some ice cream and were enjoying the warm summer evening. Around the corner from our house we came upon a group of their friends so we took a few minutes to visit. There was an open Jeep vehicle that had stopped in the street with a father and daughter sitting inside, and some of the kids were gathered around the daughter's side of the vehicle. As I watched the kids interact something odd caught my attention. The driver of the Jeep had black sunglasses on when it was dark outside, but that was not all. He just sat there and stared through the windshield of the vehicle, chin up and stoic, never moving his head, never saying a word, never a part of what was going on around him. He was like a droid. The effect was obvious. Everything about his daughter was screaming for attention. He was present, but not there.

A prison inmate was speaking with a pastor and told him an interesting truth about life on the inside of a penitentiary. He said that on Mother's Day there was always a waiting line to use the phones, but on Father's Day you could pick any phone you wanted, they were all open. It is reasonable to believe this condition started before the confinement began. In other words, the abandonment did not start when the men went to prison, it started some time before. A high percentage of inmates are there for crimes related to addiction, so we can also understand that under the surface there are struggles with dependency as well. Whether these conditions for inmates came as a result of the decisions of the father or the son is irrelevant, because that would only produce blame. Maybe the father abandoned the son, or perhaps the son abandoned the father, possibly both. Each situation can be different. But the fact that being abandoned by others leads to problems is more to the point. Could it be that disruptions in our relationships with our earthly fathers produce dependency problems with our Heavenly Father? The answer is yes, and the outcome is called codependency, for both men and women.

There are many ways that we can be abandoned by other people, which can certainly lead to disruptions in our dependence upon close relationships. Unresolved issues will come out eventually, such as a codependent that knows how to show a good face in public, then go home and vent anger on the family. They often blame their emotional outburst on the family, similar to the addict blaming the family for their drinking and drug use. This is a reflection of immature emotions and probably stems from past issues more than the current circumstances. Children raised in this type of environment are the same ones who blame themselves for their parent's divorce, a trait they learned by watching.

Taking responsibility for things we are not responsible for is also an issue for most codependents. Sometimes this comes in the form of taking blame for another person's failures or taking credit for someone else's success. People who are abandoned by others will learn this type of external focus, by depending on something outside of themselves to provide internal validation, or in some cases condemnation. It comes from a void that exists inside the person, one that only God can fill. Codependency will lead people to fill the void left by the abandonment of another person with unhealthy dependence. The truth is we all have this type of void in our lives, just in different degrees. How we fill it will determine whether we find healthy dependence or not. Codependents who try to fill this void with other people will continue the cycle of abandonment by others, because they will ruin relationships. Some people have a long history of repeating this pattern, never understanding that they are the ones who keep it going.

It is also very common to find people in general, and codependents in particular, who make strong statements about how they are going to take a stand with someone, only to avoid the conversation or cave in when given the chance. This brings together the issues of abandonment and codependency, being afraid that other people are going to quit if good boundaries are established. People are often afraid to set limits when somebody else is taking advantage of them, disrespecting them, or denying their need for healthy change. They want to stand firm but do not, because based on past experience they are afraid the other person will abandon them.

One very powerful phone call I once received came from a codependent seeking help. She had finally discovered what her struggles had been for years, why she had recurring problems with relationships. She was tired of people "quitting on her." She said her problem was codependency, but when she went to her pastor she was told that the subject was just a word for television talk shows. Her discovery of truth was dismissed as a lie. During the call she expressed her difficulty in having been at this church since her youth and wanting to stay, but knowing she didn't have support for the solution to her problems. This woman was stuck in a generational obligation to a church that she really did not want to be a part of. That is why she called — looking for help to do the very thing her conscience was telling her to do, while her codependency was talking her out of it. In a sense she was being abandoned by others, those who would not recognize her condition or need for codependent recovery.

Taking the right steps is usually simple, but rarely easy. Do not expect a person to be happy about the changes one needs to make, especially if he/she becomes accustomed to one's lack of boundaries. If making healthy choices causes people to abandon a person, then what was there to hold onto in the first place? It could be that the deep level of intimacy one thought existed was really shallow all along. "*Uncovering the truth does not produce the problem, it only exposes it.*" People who love and care about a person might see the need to adjust when someone makes changes, but they will not quit, because they value the relationship. This is the example of Christ, upon whom we depend deeply and intimately, knowing He never quits or gives up on us.

Lastly, we have examples of when two people come together with matching broken parts and it seems like a match made in heaven. Conversations about how much they understand each other are translated into some magical spiritual God-ordained blessing, when it is really about having matching broken parts that are damaged. Codependency will show it is the answer that one has been dreaming of. This explains why codependents tend to marry "projects" instead of partners, needing something external to fixed. The truth is it leads to abandonment when the project will not cooperate.

Dialogue of Addiction

A hypothetical dialogue will help to understand how addiction, codependency, and abandonment fit together. In this discussion, some "typical" comments and responses are used that provide insights, as well as exposing the nature of some common statements. Each of these statements shows a common characteristic of addiction and codependency in parenthesis. Afterwards there is a commentary explaining how the dialogue applies to abandonment. This conversation uses the classic example of a male addict or alcoholic who is married to a female codependent, however these concepts can be applied regardless of gender.

> Addict: "I feel worthless; using (drugs) will make me feel better." (abandoned)
> Codependent: "I cannot believe he did this to me. Can't he see how much this hurts the family and me? Obviously not, I will make sure he knows." (controller)
> Addict: "I wish she would get off my back and leave me alone. Besides, if you had a wife like mine you would drink too, and I am not hurting anyone but myself." (selfish)
> Codependent: "Can't he see that I am trying to help him? With all that I do for him, and this is the thanks I get." (Martyr)
> Addict: "If I were a good enough person she would not try to fix me. I feel worthless; using (drugs) will make me feel better." (abandoned)
> And the cycle repeats…

In this dialogue both the addict and the codependent experience abandonment. When the addict uses drugs they are abandoning the value of who God made them to be, and are pursuing a cheap and worthless feel good experience. The codependent is abandoning their God-given identity and purpose in life just to chase the addict. Continuing the lifestyle for the codependent does not lead to peace or acceptance. Typically the person locked in this cycle is full of anxiety and fear, are stressed out, cannot sleep and can't take anymore. Codependents will eventually find themselves alone just like the addict, or desperately pursuing one relationship after another. It is pure abandonment and self-destruction, all the while denying that they are the cause of their own problems.

The codependent controller in the dialogue is self-focused, because everything is stated as it relates to her. She is trying to control the addiction of the other person while at the same time making it about herself, proven by the statement "I cannot believe he did this to me," as if it was ever about her in the first place. Taking responsibility for things we are not responsible for is an issue of codependency.

In the second statement by the addict, he has gone from being abandoned to being selfish under the false belief that he is not hurting anybody, which is total denial. Test that by putting a name and a face to every person affected by the addict's addiction; there will be many. How can a person who is hurting so many people deny that it is taking place? They do this through selfish abandonment of truth. The dialogue also ties together addiction and codependency in the same person, when the addict blames the wife for his problems. Anything could be substituted in the statement of having "a wife like mine." It could be a "job like mine," or a family, a car, or even a "day like mine." Blaming dysfunctional behavior on someone else is more about codependency than addiction.

The codependent's next response is genuine love being masked in dysfunctional codependency. It is like running spring water through a dirty filter, where something that is pure and clean will come out polluted. What is the real motive behind trying to help? If it is really about helping the other person, then it will not have a condition attached. When the codependent provides conditional help, such as help that comes with the expectation of gratitude, then there is a price attached which is not based on genuine love and concern, but control and manipulation. It is actually playing God in the life of another person. Eventually it becomes a roadblock to successful healing; a person cannot help in a Godly manner while at the same time playing the role of a martyr.

This type of lifestyle is where the problem of codependency continues to grow through the experiences of the relationship. A problem that is not addressed will always get worse. As the cycle continues to repeat itself, the problems progress for both parties. What codependents need to understand is that trying to control the life of an addict leads not to gratitude, but bitterness, frustration, and anger. The real issue for the addict is they actually do not like being treated as an incompetent person, but they are willing to go along with the program if the codependent will enable and rescue them. The combination of anger and accepting enabling will lead to extreme conditions, and when it all fails the addicts will feel worthless about themselves.

For the codependent this validates the role of martyr because people are not grateful for their contribution, but the truth is they set the circumstances up in the first place by the way they tried to help. One of the most difficult things to get a codependent to understand is their part of the problem. For both people represented in this dialogue, the outcome is they will move from being abandoned by others to abandoning themselves.

Abandoned by Ourselves

"*Addictive, compulsive, or codependent behavior is an abandonment of ourselves.*" Believing we have no value gives us permission to destroy either relationships or ourselves. This develops into a search for someone or something to fix the problem, which instead of making a person whole will actually cause fragmentation of the inner self. Trying to fix brokenness with addiction and codependency results in more brokenness. There are no perfect people; we all have some degree of this problem. For some it is just the reality of living in a world with problems, but for others it becomes a repeated pattern that is self-destructive.

An analogy that works to describe this condition is that of an internal "calculator." Let's say that we are all born with a calculator inside of us that just has a few buttons. Through our experiences we will develop and add more buttons that will increasingly be used to make decisions in life. Babies quickly learn to use one of the few buttons they have: cry and throw a fit. When they are hungry, wet, or tired they just simply use what they have available. The goal is for the display to show the correct results, which as an infant this is just to be "happy." As we grow older we will need more mature results than just expecting to be happy all the time.

More buttons are added as we grow through either nurturing or neglect. The type of buttons will be determined by our experiences and how we are taught to respond to life. Going into adolescence a person needs certain buttons to make good choices. Without them the only options available are immature, like crying and throwing a fit, options that do not meet the challenges. These might have worked well when the diaper was wet, but not for the challenges facing a teenager.

Eventually we arrive at adulthood with a variety of "buttons"; some people will have more, some less. If abuse was part of our developing years, we will have buttons that were put there by the sin of someone else. Whatever degree of love and nurturing we experience will produce positive buttons, maybe just a few, maybe a lot. Each person is similar in many regards but different in what they have to function with. Some have healthy buttons, others have unhealthy ones, but most people have a blend of both. Much of it depends on the degree of Godly examples we had in our lives.

For some of us buttons were added that should not be there, at least not according to God's plan for our lives. The temptations of life produce opportunity, and some people received help from others to add buttons such as "smoke this" or "drink that." Perhaps it was "take this" and feel better. That is exactly what the display on the calculator reads for a young boy or girl who gets high or drunk, "feel better." It works, and becomes a predictable, repeatable, and pleasurable experience. Progressively more buttons are added to the calculator that represent an increase in the types and amounts of drugs and alcohol, but still the display reads, "feel better."

For others, buttons were forced upon their calculator by a codependent parent. The "walk on eggshells" button is familiar to this child. For them having a blank display is the best possible result, because denying reality is better than accepting it. Parents who do not allow their children to use their own calculator to make age appropriate decisions will produce young adults who do not know how to make good decisions. For these children it was always bad to make decisions, so that is exactly what they learned, to avoid using their own calculator and trust the display. They will try to cheat, by looking at other people's calculators to decide how they should feel or act, because it is what they learned to do. They become externally focused to find identity, searching in all the wrong places for a display that reads, "loved." A few common buttons used by this person will be labeled "fight" or "flight."

Then one day a familiar button is pushed and it no longer works. The display reads "pain" and it does not feel good anymore. At this point a person can recognize the broken nature of their calculator and change direction. Not so for the addict, who is driven to try different types of substances, taken in different ways, with increasing effects. But the display just continues to read "pain." Over and over and over they try to change the buttons but the results stay the same. They are looking for the old result and cannot find it, yet the search continues. They will try to recreate the "good old days" but will never find them. Codependents will repeat learned patterns in their adult relationships to feel better, but cannot get away from the result of continued pain. They use relationships like addicts use drugs, to get their fix and feel better. If they have passed these conditions onto their children, they will find the loneliness that comes from being abandoned by their adult children. A codependent parent with a broken calculator will continue trying to use the buttons that worked when the children were young, trying desperately to get the same results. They will be driven to try different types of control or manipulation, but the display will continue to read "pain."

Why do addicts and codependents keep doing the same thing over and over expecting a different result (commonly referred to as the definition of insanity)? They are missing buttons that were never added and do not have recovery as a choice yet. Codependents who do not allow consequences for others have put themselves in the way of God entering the equation. They interrupt the process of sowing and reaping by enabling or rescuing, and then wonder why it does not produce good results in the life of another person. It is like having a "control" button on the calculator that is installed but not functioning, just giving the appearance of having control but without results.

During some of the time I worked in manufacturing, my job was to install and maintain the controls for the production lines. In one area a problem arose with people changing the setting for the equipment and causing problems with the daily results. It was one of those situations where trying to "fix" a problem that did not exist was actually causing problems. It seemed that everyone knew how to solve "the problem" and they all had different ideas. After months of asking for cooperation with no success, I came up with a solution. An adjustable knob known as a "potentiometer" was installed, and it could be adjusted to certain settings. A sign was placed over the knob asking workers to make their adjustments using this device only. It was changed constantly and even had small pencil marks to show the preferred settings. Several times per shift the knob was adjusted by various people to fix the problem and improve the outcome. The truth however is it had wires coming off the back making it look just like a real device, but they just disappeared into the groups of other wires and remained unconnected. It was not a functioning device, it had no connection to the operating system, but provided the appearance of control and everyone was happy.

That is how codependents function in relationships using their internal calculator, thinking they have control over things they have no control over, but believing they do. Every day they will use the same buttons to manipulate the outcome, happy that it is all going their way when nothing is really going their way, it is just a delusion. They will constantly focus outside themselves, trying to "fix" problems that do not exist, and in doing so will cause problems. Some codependents live like this for years and decades, pushing their "control" button with a false sense of results. Their conscience, the internal device that God provided, will be present but disconnected and not functioning. Their display will read "happy," but they will never really be satisfied or content.

At this stage, when either the addict or codependent have the opportunity to realize they are broken inside, a new direction can be taken to avoid further damage. If not, they will continue their lifestyle and experience more damage. This could very well describe the line that people cross where they go from substance abuser to full-blown addict, or mild codependent to flaming. One thing is for sure: if a person chooses not to face the truth and runs from the solution, the problem will get worse, never better.

An example from the Bible is when the nation of Israel was set free from Egypt. They followed God's plan, and eventually came to the bank of the Jordan River. Numbers Chapters 13 and 14 record a critical mistake made by the Israelites: they chose not to cross the river and enter into the Promised Land. The excuses were pitiful in light of God's promises, but they chose to avoid it anyway. The story records how they protested against Moses and were afraid of the challenges. Seems their calculators still had some old familiar buttons, which produced the old familiar results. Even though they had been provided with new choices they still did not trust. The result was consequences, pain, and suffering. After wandering through the desert for 40 years they came back to the same place at the Jordan River. That is what happens to people who get a chance to face their problems and refuse. They will eventually find that they have wandered in life, gone in circles, and wound up right back where they were before.

So how does recovery help these conditions? It takes place when an experienced person comes into the picture and is able to say, "You have a calculator like mine, the one I used to have, but yours is still broken and defective. It does not have any solution buttons and needs repair." The experienced person shows the newcomer what to add first to their calculator. In recovery there are buttons like "go to meetings, work the steps, read the book, make phone calls, and help others with the same problem." If the newcomer is willing to surrender to the truth about their broken calculator, there is hope. Otherwise they will ignore advice, refuse to listen, and just keep trying the same old things with the same old buttons, but the results will get worse never better. They say that recovery will ruin your drinking. Once you know that your calculator is broke, you can try to deny it but the truth is known.

The use of this analogy when entering recovery is like trying to use a scientific calculator when you have not even mastered one with basic equations. Perhaps there are buttons that were available but never used or were ignored, or they were used for all the wrong reasons and became dysfunctional. Surrendering your will and life over to God's care might seem complicated, but it is not. The addict needs someone to show them how to use the new buttons, and so does the codependent. Those with experience teach others how to work the new tools, which are sometimes confusing but require listening, following directions, and not trying to figure it out on your own. When a person begins to crumble, break down, and fragment inside, the desire to reach for the old solutions will be strong. They were predictable even though they were defective. The new solutions are confusing, but they work.

As people grow and learn to trust God and others, they will also realize that the spiritual section of the calculator has a button labeled "Son of God." You push it when you are ready to accept Jesus Christ into your life. There are also examples of people who push this button first, and find healing in ways that do not include recovery groups or processes. Both will eventually be faced with the temptation to use the old buttons. They will stay on the right path if they do not abandon the new buttons, and will find that instead of pain the display reads "peace."

"And the peace of God, which transcends all understanding, will guard your hearts and your minds in Christ Jesus." Phil. 4:7.

When experienced people in recovery say, "Let go and let God," it might sound desirable but confusing. Codependents have a tendency to hold onto their broken calculator because they are convinced that only the addict's calculator is broke, theirs is just fine. *"It is only through the admission of brokenness that a soul can find healing."* Fragmentation is the same as brokenness. Each time a person pushes the old predictable button, there is a fracture in the inner person. The addict gets high, and the codependent tries to control the uncontrollable. Either way, it causes pain and suffering. Both will often accuse others of "pushing their buttons" as an attempt to make excuses for bad behavior. It is really not possible for other people to do this without giving them the access in the first place. We have a choice, and we are responsible for our own choices.

This analogy ultimately shows how you can experience abandonment without anybody else's participation. We abandon the life God intended for us and accept a cheap alternative. Whether addressing an addiction or codependency, the acceptance of brokenness and the need for healing has to take place. For most people it happens because they see the reality of what their choices in life have brought them to, and change. That change almost always, with few exceptions, involves three parties: God, ourselves, and another person. We stop abandoning ourselves, and accept the value that God has placed on our lives, an act of surrender.

Abandoned by God

We may have been abandoned by others, and surely have some level of abandonment of ourselves, but what about God? Never, at least while on this earth. Hebrews 13:5 is a re-statement of Joshua 1:5, which states, *"I will never leave you nor forsake you."* Many if not all of the descriptions of codependency from chapter two will struggle with this principle. In their minds they will believe that God will never abandon them, but their hearts only know conditional love that creates doubts. People pleasers, perfectionists, and those who live with false guilt and shame, all will doubt their spiritual security.

This false belief that God will abandon us comes from not being able to separate behavior from identity, which is exactly what God is able to do. He will respond to our behavior both good and bad, but His love for us remains consistent based on our identity. Sin entered into this world as a result of Adam and Eve's behavior, but God still loved them because of their identity. God did not abandon them; He made a provision for them, just like He makes provisions for us. In the garden Adam and Eve were ashamed because of something related to their behavior. God provided clothes for them because of their identity, not because they deserved it, but because of whom they were. The consequences they did receive were because of their behavior. Sin then entered the world, and today we have behavior problems called addiction and codependency. We don't deserve it, but because of our identity,

God provided a solution that man called 12-step recovery. He will never leave us, nor forsake us.

Ron E. #9 is a man who served his country as a veteran of World War II. He was seriously injured in combat in Germany during the war and returned home as a disabled vet. Many surgeries, a metal plate in his head, and a lengthy period of rehabilitation lay ahead. Many years later he became a widower, and lived out his final days as a resident of a Veterans Home. He was not able to go to the ball field or the pool that was available, but could get around the living quarters and to the chow hall. He was confined to the grounds of the vets home for safety reasons.

There were times during the height of my own drug use that I actually wanted to kill Ron E. #9, for what he did to me as a child who trusted him. He was my grandfather, and a pedophile. After a long and successful life of molesting and sexually abusing his family, he was confronted and promised to stop but did not. At the age of 70 he reoffended and finally faced criminal charges. Instead of prison he was confined to the Veterans Home. The reason he could not go to the ball field or pool was because children might be there. He also could not leave the grounds because he was a danger to society. He had spent a lifetime hiding behind the sympathy of his injured veteran status, but the consequences finally caught up with him.

After entering recovery from alcohol and drug addiction I had to face the resentments and pains of my past. Biblical reconciliation is required for successful recovery. Naturally my grandfather made the list of resentments as my hatred for him was strong. I found other people easier to forgive, but not him. Several years went by and I was experiencing blessings beyond measure in my life. I had come to understand the Gospel and had opened my heart to Christ, as well as remaining clean and sober without relapsing. But the hatred towards my grandfather remained and after several years it was time for it to go.

The struggle was figuring out how to approach the whole situation. Recovery had taught me to make direct amends whenever possible, but what would I make amends for when I was truly the victim of a sick man? This subject had always been the family secret, no one ever talked about it. It became my own source of shame, so I never discussed it. I decided that the best way to approach the problem was to go see him face-to-face and tell him that I had forgiven him. Doing the right thing is not always easy; sometimes it is the hardest thing to do. Genuine forgiveness was not an overnight matter, I had to pray and ask God for help. He reminded me that His son was abused by people, and still forgave. Dependence upon right from wrong based on God's standards was crucial. I would have never taken action without it.

So I went to the vets home one day along with my mother. We all had lunch together and then walked back towards the dorm. Mom knew why we were there, and at a prearranged time she left us and went to the car. I faced my grandfather, looked him straight in the eye and said, "I came here today to tell you that I forgive you for what you did to me when I was a young child." The next couple of minutes seemed like the equivalent of Moses seeing the burning bush that was not consumed. I was stunned. Suddenly there was person talking to me that I had never met before. My grandfather had always been in his own world, never quite present in the moment, his head in the clouds somewhere. That was just normal for him, but not at that moment. He looked at me as a completely different person, both his tone of voice and facial appearance changed, and then said, "I am so sorry for what I did to you, I hate myself, and I am so sorry." Tears were running down his face as he continued to apologize. For just a couple of minutes we talked as two genuine people, and then I saw it start to happen. The distant look started coming back, his tone of voice began to change, the fogged over look appeared, and he was gone. I watched in amazement as he just said "thanks for lunch," turned around and walked away.

Later that night I was at home writing in my journal about the experience. There was a moment when everything came clear. With the hatred gone God was teaching me something, and I wrote it down. *"The addiction covers my true identity so I don't have to look at it. God's love embraces my true identity so I can look at it and accept it, both good and bad. Satan's lie, 'You won't surely die.' The pleasures of addiction do cause death, death to the experience of our true identity and God's love. Abandonment of self for something is of little value."*

What I came to understand about my grandfather was that for one moment of one day, I actually met the real person. It was buried so deep within him that it never saw the light of day, covered by a lifetime of spiritual, emotional, mental, and physical sickness. And before we get too high and mighty about ourselves, remember that the difference between him and us might just be the type of sickness and the time spent living in it. Does the addict or the codependent cause any less damage in the lives of those who love them? Is their true identity buried underneath layers of pretense, image, and trying to hide from the truth? Is that you? Did you buy the lie? Do you think that because you did not physically die from codependency that nothing else did?

Codependents are people who trade the truth for a lie, and abandon all that God created them to be. Our true identity is more than a principle to learn; it is critical to overcoming codependency. The application is incredibly simple, but must be preceded by learning the difference between identity and behavior according to the Bible.

What is our true identity? First we have to understand that we are created in God's image (Gen. 1:27). *"So God created mankind in his own image, in the image of God he created them; male and female, he created them."* This applies to all mankind regardless of where you were born or the color of your skin. All human beings are created in the image of God. Next, we have the choice to accept Jesus Christ as our Savior, the atonement or sacrifice for our sins. This does not apply to all mankind; it is a choice that each person makes. When we take this step the Holy Spirit comes and lives within our hearts as a result of believing in Christ. God identifies us as His children as a result of believing the Gospel and accepting Jesus Christ as our Lord and Savior.

"*Now it is God who makes both us and you stand firm in Christ. He anointed us, set his seal of ownership on us, and put his Spirit in our hearts as a deposit, guaranteeing what is to come.*" II Corinthians 1:21-22.

"*The Spirit himself testifies with our spirit that we are God's children.*" Romans 8:16.

"*And you also were included in Christ when you heard the message of truth, the gospel of your salvation. When you believed, you were marked in him with a seal, the promised Holy Spirit,*" Ephesians 1:13.

"*Yet to all who did receive him, to those who believed in his name, he gave the right to become children of God — children born not of natural descent, nor of human decision or a husband's will, but born of God.*" John 1:13-14.

"*For it is by grace you have been saved, through faith, and this is not from yourselves, it is the gift of God — not by works, so that no one can boast.*" Ephesians 2:8-9.

Jesus explained all this to Nicodemus in John Chapter 3. He told the seeking Pharisee that he "must be born again." Confused by the idea, Jesus had to explain further

"*Flesh gives birth to flesh, but the spirit gives birth to spirit. You should not be surprised at my saying, 'You must be born again.'*" John 3:6-7.

- To be born of the flesh is to be born in the image of God.
- To be born of the Spirit is to make a decision to accept Jesus Christ as Savior.
- Then the Holy Spirit comes and lives within us, and we become children of God.

The following is my explanation of God's method for validating our Salvation Card, taking our identity of being born in His image and combining it with our identity of being born again as children of God.

In heaven, there is a book called the Lamb's Book of Life. In it are written the names of the people that are going to heaven. In order to get your name in the book, you have to be perfect. We have a problem. We all have a problem. We are all sinners, and it only takes one sin to not have your name written in that book. We needed a way to get our names written in that Book. Jesus said, "I am the way, the truth, and the life; no man comes to the Father but by me." John 14:6. There is nothing you can do to earn your way into heaven. It is an insolvable problem, but Jesus Christ solved the problem.

When He died on the cross He paid the penalty for our sins, and three days later when He rose from the grave He gained the victory over death to give us eternal life. That is the Gospel, it is the truth. You can accept it or reject it, it is up to you. But to enter heaven you not only have to trust in something outside of yourself, which is Christ Himself, but you also have to invite Him in. Because every knee is going to bow, "in heaven, and on earth, and under the earth." Phil. 2:10. You can do it now or do it later, but later is too late. The decision to accept the Gospel has to be made before you die.

John 3:16 states, "God so loved the world that he gave his one and only Son, that whoever believes in him shall not perish but have everlasting life." The "world" is you because the only part of creation that God wants to save is the souls of human beings. Everything else will pass away.

If you want to make a decision, the terms are simple: just believe and ask. The words can vary as long as the message isn't changed. One example would be:

"Lord Jesus, I am a sinner and I cannot change myself. I believe that you died for my sins, and that you rose from the dead to give me eternal life. I ask you to forgive me and come into my

heart as my Savior. I trust that my name will be written in your Book of Life. Thank you for loving me. Amen".

If you made the decision and accepted God's plan of salvation, then there is a lot of rejoicing taking place right now. Share your decision with someone else that can not only rejoice with you, but also be a support and encouragement to you as a child of God.

Jesus himself said, "I tell you, there is rejoicing in the presence of the angels of God over one sinner who repents." Luke 15:10.

One person from the Old Testament who certainly understood his identity was King David. He was a great man of God, yet he failed many times. As a youth he depended on God's power; as an adult, he turned to his own lustful desires. David was far from a perfect person, but he clearly understood the difference between his identity and his behavior. God used David to write many of the Psalms, but one is probably the most recognized, Psalm 23.

> *The* LORD *is my shepherd, I shall not want.*
> *He makes me lie down in green pastures, He leads me*
>   *beside still waters,*
> *He restores my soul.*
> *He leads me in the paths of righteousness for His name's*
>   *sake.*
> *Even though I walk through the valley of the shadow of*
>   *death,*
> *I will fear no evil, for you are with me;*
> *your rod and your staff, they comfort me.*
> *You prepare a table before me in the presence of my ene-*
>   *mies;*
> *You anoint my head with oil; my cup overflows.*
> *Surely goodness and mercy will follow me all the days of*
>   *my life,*
> *and I will dwell in the house of the* LORD *forever.* (ESV)

The shepherd cares for his flock. Even when one strays into trouble he comforts and protects them. He prepares good things for them. His goodness and love follow them, it pursues them. God will pursue after us with goodness and love, even when we stray into trouble. God will never abandon one of His children. But codependency will lead to performance-based identity, being externally focused in a constantly changing world, trading good for bad, living in the extremes of an identity without balance. *"Abandonment has to take place before codependency can exist."* Simple acceptance of God's truth will correct this condition.

- Identity based on behavior will fail.
- Identity based on being human will change.
- Identity based on the character of God will remain consistent while on earth and for eternity.

Identity vs. behavior means you can make mistakes and know in your heart that God will still love and protect you unconditionally. In John 8:31 Jesus said, *"If you hold to my teaching, you are truly my disciples. Then you will know the truth, and the truth will set you free."* Being free from abandonment is achieved when you know that your identity as a child of God is secure, that He will *"never leave you nor forsake you."* Hebrews 13:5. If abandonment has to take place before codependency can exist, then resolving issues of abandonment will provide healing from codependency as well.

Are you ready to explore the fog?

CHAPTER

4

There is Something in the Fog

I n the 1980's there was a movie titled "The Fog," in which the lead character uses her radio program to warn others there was something in the fog that was engulfing a small town. The film centered on the idea that something scary was living in the fog people could not see, but it was going to eventually cause them harm. Most of the movie revolved around running away from whatever was in the fog, until it was identified, confronted, and defeated.

Every human being has some degree of issue with the fog, meaning the ability to clearly and perfectly see their own internal issues. It comes as a result of being an imperfect person raised by imperfect people in an imperfect world. In other words, *"all have sinned and come short of the glory of God."* Romans 3:10. It is also true that no two people have exactly the same amount of fog, even though we often have the same type. Multiple children raised in the same home can have different degrees, but the type they live in can have common characteristics. The important point to understand is that *"there is something in the fog"*; we cannot see it, but we are running from it. It can eventually cause us harm unless it is identified, confronted, and defeated.

We learn and accumulate most of this condition while growing up. For some people it creates minor challenges, life-threatening issues for others. Some people live in the fog all their lives, consumed with a false sense of identity that goes all the way back to their childhood and family of origin. This condition is not rare or hard to find. It can exist in individuals and institutions, can be passed down generationally, and will be an influence for better or for worse. Another important characteristic is that no one is predestined to stay in the fog. We have choices as individuals that can change the course of our lives, which will have a tremendous impact on what kind of fog we pass down to the next generation.

So, what is it that lives in the fog? For most people what lives within are the negative and harmful influences in their emotions, thinking, and spirituality. Its connection to codependency is in the destructive forms of dependence that are created by the fog. For example, when a person feels obligated to a role in life or belief system that was established in their family, he/she can feel guilty for not following the program, experience shame for not living up to the expectations, and even live with self-condemnation because he/she may have never confronted and defeated these false beliefs. This can either set up a lifetime of frustration without clarity, or present the opportunity to confront the problems. The truth is we will never completely rid ourselves of the fog, but we can absolutely find clarity, heal from the destructive influences, and not pass it on to our families. But we must first identify what lives inside the fog that is causing us harm.

All of the common themes of codependency apply to the analogy of the fog: externally focused, role reversal, all-or-nothing extremes, abandonment, and validation. There is definitely something in the fog. It can be a problem for those who avoid their issues as well as those who try to control them. It can make mountains out of molehills, or deny that a molehill is actually a mountain. The fog can make people hold on to their pain, because it is easier than confronting and defeating the source. It can hold issues of shame, guilt, or the trauma of abuse. Recovery from codependency takes place when people stop running, defending, and blaming and face whatever is in the fog.

This principle relates to the story of the pastor's wife in Russia from Chapter One. She was the wife of a minister, mother of three, and completely discouraged in life. Her prayers had been answered for a good husband and family, so she felt guilty for being discouraged. She was obligating herself to a role that had been predetermined while growing up. Her passion was to be a Mary Kay Director, but she lived in the fog of believing that her sole purpose in life was to take care of her husband, children and nothing more. She was starting to resent her role and it was affecting her relationship with the family. Her codependency was holding on to what was bad and trying to make it good, and she was close to abandoning her passion. Validation as a good wife and mother was not solving the problem, so even her pre-determined role was becoming dysfunctional. The whole problem existed in the fog of false expectations, ones that were being placed on her by herself.

While meeting with her and her husband, we listed on paper what her life would look like being a good wife, mother, and a director. These three roles became the new goal to work towards. Sometimes it is not this simple to clear out the fog, but that really doesn't matter; the main point is finding clarity. Whatever is in the fog will keep a person from his/her passion in life.

Defining what lives in the fog is the challenge for each individual. Even though there are common issues, they will have varying degrees. For example, if two people that are unrelated both grew up with alcoholic parents, their issues will be similar in nature but different in their experiences. This is where a common mistake is made: people believe that no one understands, and no one else has the same problems. This is a half-truth that is produced by focusing externally on the details of another person's life. A codependent will be quick to find the differences and slow to find the similarities. If another person had alcoholic parents, but had a different geographical location, income level, ethnic background, vocation, etc., then the codependent would use these differences to claim their own uniqueness. This is another way to avoid what is in the fog. As humans we are more common than we are unique.

Codependents live in a fantasy world. The control they think they have over others is not real, especially when they do not even have control over themselves. People will think they have done well with their children, only to experience rejection by the children when they become adults. A parent who is still living in the fog will not understand why the rejection is taking place, and resort to blame, rage, or being a victim. This will only serve to increase the rejection as time goes on, unless the parent stops claiming their uniqueness and confronts whatever is hiding in the fog.

In recovery the fog most often represents "family of origin" issues. Underneath the layers of behaviors and attitudes are the influences of the developing years, when the emotional, mental, and spiritual health were supposed to be developing at the same time that our physical body was growing. We have similarities and differences in the families we grew up with. This is true whether a person grew up in a healthy environment or a dysfunctional one, a first family or a blended family, with their birth parents or in an orphanage. All will have some degree of fog that was produced by our family of origin. *"Trying to find uniqueness from the differences only leads to isolation."*

The Bible has plenty to say about the family of origin, but also adoption into God's family. Much of the scriptures are devoted to recording the lineage of God's people, from the "begats" of Genesis to the Genealogy of Christ in Matthew Chapter One. Jesus' earthly family of origin was very important, because it had to include a virgin mother, the Holy Spirit, and a human father who was His stepfather. Lineage is important to God, as it represents the generations of family. He also wants us to know that we can be adopted into His family through faith in Jesus Christ.

This does not mean that we lose our human family or origin, but that we gain a spiritual family. The nature of this principle helps people find healing from what exists in the fog, because we do not have to separate from our family of origin or try to avoid the truth about it. We just have to bring clarity by accepting God's plan for facing the past and defeating its influence. *"All of us are spiritual orphans who need to be adopted into our Heavenly Father's family."*

If the fog is going to be cleared then some specific work has to be done on the issue of shame. This issue can be so intoxicating that it causes people to lose all sound judgment and make impaired decisions. It can paralyze a person from taking action when they need to, especially in the area of abuse. People who are experiencing the trauma of current or past abuse will determine to take a stand, but will stop short of taking action and feel shame for not doing so. Shame can cause a codependent to never develop loving dependent relationships that are intimate, the very thing they desire. It will also disrupt their relationship with God, because life becomes about behavior instead of identity.

A study of the word "shame" or "ashamed" from the Old and New Testaments shows these words are often translated as "confusion" or "confused." There are other times when they are translated twisted, distorted, or perverse. Knowing when and how to apply the different uses of the words will help in the healing process. If a person is actually confused about their identity, but are experiencing it as distorted or perverse, then the shame they feel will remain hidden in their heart, inside of the fog. People who try to be perfectionist will have this experience. They are never satisfied, no matter what. If things are going good, they are not good enough. Trying to address perfectionism without connecting it to the sources of shame will only lead to temporary satisfaction. Just pulling the weed without removing the root will allow it to grow again.

Christians who are entering recovery will face this issue on a particular level, because they will have to reconcile why their faith in Christ did not produce results with addiction or codependency. This will be shameful in the sense of confusion, which comes from not understanding the problems or avoiding the solution. It is not a perverse application of shame, there is nothing twisted about it. A person who knows God but is a dysfunctional codependent is confused.

In Genesis 2:25, "*Adam and his wife were both naked, and they felt no shame.*" They were not confused about being naked; nothing was wrong and it was how God intended it to be, pure and acceptable. This was the condition before sin entered into the picture, when they depended on God to keep things in balance. There was no confusion. There was no shame. It was only after they went against God and chose independence over dependence that shame occurred. They became confused and tried to hide their problem, much like people today try to hide their codependency behind religious behaviors.

An example of the other definition of shame is in Psalm 4:2 — "*How long will you people turn my glory into shame? How long will you love delusions and seek false gods?*" This scripture is an example of shame that is distorted or perverse. Turning God's glory into shame is what happens when role reversal is used, by taking something that is good such as God's glory and turning it into something bad and shameful. Codependents will try to find exception with the idea that they are turning God's glory into something bad, while at the same time holding tight to the delusions which are causing chaos in their lives. Enablers that are interfering with the process of reaping and sowing will see themselves as helping and having compassion, but violating God's Word will only lead them to shame. "*There is definitely a fine line between compassion and enabling,*" just as there is a fine line between shame that is confusion and that which is distorted, perverse, and delusional. The fog will blind a person from knowing when they have crossed the line.

Seeing shame as confusion is not a way to shed responsibility. It is a way to understand that who we are in God's eyes has been damaged by life's experiences, leaving confusion that reveals itself in the form of shame. If applying the truth about shame as confusion leads to more confusion, then we will just become perpetual victims blaming the circumstances of life for our shame. Instead, we accept the good and the bad of our experiences. The shame we feel for the bad experiences can be understood as confusion caused by the influences of a sinful world. Nothing can change until we take responsibility for the condition of our lives. God then becomes the focus as the source of truth, because if we blame Him for allowing bad things to happen, then we remain confused and influenced by shame. Accepting this does not make the wrong right, or the pain justified, it simply transforms sin into grace. What has been a curse can become a blessing. *"To bestow on them a crown of beauty instead of ashes, the oil of joy instead of mourning, and a garment of praise instead of a spirit of despair."* Isaiah 61:3.

When we are ready to accept our lives as they are, then we are ready to surrender our way of solving our own problems. Arriving at this place motivates us to seek God and trust in Him to remove the fog. We can accept that *"unresolved shame has lead to unhealthy dependency, which leads to codependency."* Often this is where the codependent realizes that shame has been both a powerful and destructive tool because it has the power to control others while at the same time it causes damage to personal relationships. Trying to sort all of this out without the help of God and others only leads to more confusion, and ultimately back around to the same problem. The more severe problems often require professional help. Active participation in a church or recovery program can meet these needs.

The issues common to most people can be combined into three statements: the fog, family of origin and the generational transfer of shame.

- Others shame me. "What is wrong with you?"
- I shame myself. "I am not good enough."
- I shame others. "What is wrong with you?"

In this simple process we can see where shame that is based on confusion becomes toxic, as well as how easily it can be transferred through our generations. If someone hears enough how bad he/she is, then that person will believe it. The message will cause confusion that will eventually produce a distorted condition in the heart. When parents bring children into the picture, they may have the desire to be different and never be like their parents. But unless this message has been confronted and defeated it will continue. Ever wonder why people who are determined to never be like their parents become just like them? They may have never actually healed from the shame that is in the fog. They just avoided it and passed it on.

Stopping the generational transfer of shame takes place by restoring one's true identity. Since this is necessary to overcome the codependent fog, one needs to understand the effects of shame on his/her identity. The use of a diagram will explain the challenges and solutions. The picture in the diagram represents an identity in the context of three areas: outer appearance, protection, and inner heart. This diagram represents the condition that God wants us to have, a proper balance of inward and outward characteristics, along with an adequate layer of protection between these two. Following the diagram is a point-by-point breakdown of the principles.

The diagram starts with a block in the upper left area as a stand-alone item. It states that "Addictions, Compulsions, & Dependencies are ways to compensate for damaged Protection and injuries to the Inner Heart." This sets the direction for the rest of the diagram, by accepting that the issues which bring us to our knees and to the point of despair are really just the surface problems. They are only expressions of what is in the fog, not the actual cause, and are a means to compensate for a lack of focus on the root of the problems. This comment also introduces the concept of damaged protection for our inner hearts. As we go through the breakdown of the diagram, this will become a key point in understanding cause and effect when it comes to the subject of shame. The idea is that something internal has been damaged by life's experiences, and that codependency has become a way to compensate for the effects of the damage. Somehow the God-given instincts for protecting ourselves have gone awry, and the result is a heart full of shame. Repairing the protection is part of the process of healing, one that will bring permanent and lasting results. It is like a castle without walls for protection that will only remain vulnerable to attack until the walls are repaired. Compensating with false solutions will only serve to increase the vulnerability.

Take a minute to review the diagram before continuing the explanation of the principles.

Circle of Identity

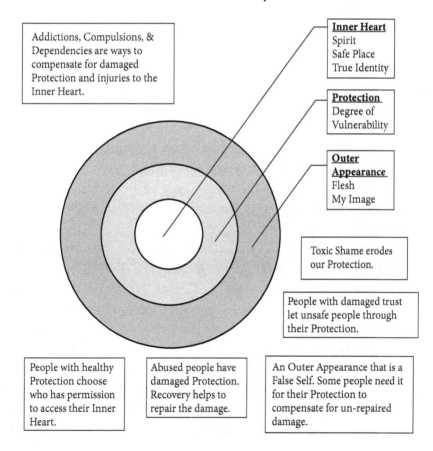

Addictions, Compulsions, & Dependencies are ways to compensate for damaged Protection and injuries to the Inner Heart.

Inner Heart
Spirit
Safe Place
True Identity

Protection
Degree of
Vulnerability

Outer Appearance
Flesh
My Image

Toxic Shame erodes our Protection.

People with damaged trust let unsafe people through their Protection.

People with healthy Protection choose who has permission to access their Inner Heart.

Abused people have damaged Protection. Recovery helps to repair the damage.

An Outer Appearance that is a False Self. Some people need it for their Protection to compensate for un-repaired damage.

As the boxes in the upper right corner indicate, our "Inner Heart" is where spirit resides. It is supposed to be a safe place where true identity is protected. Unfortunately, experiences in life will cause the heart to be anything but a safe place, especially where abuse has occurred. The level of "Protection" is shown as the degree of vulnerability; it represents how weak or solid the protection is which keeps the heart a safe place. Weak protection will lead a person to let unsafe people into their lives, and over protected people do not let anyone in. This is a "boundary" issue. People without good boundaries let bad things come into their lives and do not protect their inner heart from bad influences. They will also let bad things come out of their heart, by saying things that should never be said.

The "Outer Appearance" is the flesh, his/her image; it is what the world around us sees. Some people get their appearance confused with their protection as a result of shame. It is common for people who have failed relationships to put increased focus on their physical appearance, trying to avoid being rejected again. Instead of healing from the pain by focusing on their true identity and the love of their Heavenly Father, they just polish up and place the emphasis in the outer appearance. Unfortunately, this only leads to attracting the wrong type of person and increases the likelihood of repeating the experience. *"Our flesh was never intended to protect our hearts from pain."*

As we move clockwise around the circle the next box indicates that "toxic shame erodes our protection." Real toxic chemicals will cause damage to whatever they come in contact with, or turn something that was originally good into something bad. In the case of protecting the heart, toxic shame can cause a great deal of damage. People, who are so shame based that it can be referred to as toxic, will have a heart full of pain. Christians with this characteristic will depend on a performance-based identity to fix the problem. They can easily become a codependent missionary to go save the world without ever healing from their shame. They can also become leaders of ministries within the church. Often they are the Killer Poodles that will let you know if you get too close or challenge them. They will attack if they feel threatened.

Ron E. #7 is a clergy who is a flaming codependent. He operates in a state of chaos with one crisis after another occupying his time. What he doesn't seem to realize is that he is the one who creates the chaos, and then blames it on the devil. It would seem that Ron E. #7 is under a constant spiritual attack; in fact he will say that he is on the front lines fighting the devil for God. The truth is that he needs the chaos to avoid facing his own emotional problems, which are often expressed in fits of rage. This could accurately be described as a state of dense fog. People around him see it clearly but Ron E. #7 is unapproachable. He is surrounded by people who will not challenge him and just agree with everything he says. Call them "yes men" or something else, it is plain dysfunctional codependency. He has mustard on his face, and those who have dared to point it out have been met with aggressive hostility, or on other occasions tears and sorrow. The bottom line is that nothing will change for Ron E. #7 until he identifies whatever is in the fog, confronts it, and defeats the true enemy that is within his own heart. Nothing can change until we take responsibility for the condition of our lives

The next box in the diagram identifies another problem with damaged protection. It states "People with damaged trust let unsafe people through their Protection." Child abuse creates damaged trust, as do acts of abuse and violence between adults. When trust is violated it affects our sense of identity; people who are true victims will have a difficult time trusting people. Other influences, such as someone you love cheating on you, will deeply impact the way you trust others. Looking at the subject of shame as it relates to "Protection" helps to understand why people sometimes behave in confusing ways.

For a couple of years I worked part time at a county detox facility. In the building next door was another program that we had a lot of interaction with, one that focused on child and adult abuse. On one occasion this program had an adult female client working with three of the female staff members on a domestic violence issue. The staff was in the middle of trying to get court documents and safe housing to protect the client from an abusive man. Suddenly, the client decided to abandon all the work that was being done and go back to the man who had been abusing her. The three women from the staff were in disbelief and did the only thing they could. They locked arms across the shoulders, kicked their feet up together like a chorus line, and in unity sung, "stand by your man."

Why did this woman go back so quickly to a man that had abused her? While the complete answer is beyond our study of shame, we can certainly see that she did not have adequate protection for her own heart. If the whole picture were known, it would most likely reveal that it was not the first time she had been abused and the damage had already occurred before she ever met this man. Maybe that is why Jesus said, *"Things that cause people to stumble are bound to come, but woe to anyone through whom they come. It would be better for them to be thrown into the sea with a millstone tied around their neck than to cause one of these little ones to stumble."* Luke 17:1-2. Abused children tend to grow up and allow abusive people in their lives because their protection has been damaged. Others build walls of isolation around themselves to keep unsafe people out, but it also keeps safe and loving people out as well. *"Codependency is often a shame-based survival skill learned in abusive families."*

A common mistake that you can see anywhere in our world is people who compensate for inner shame by focusing on the "Outer Appearance." Simply put, it becomes all about image and the flesh. As the next box in the diagram indicates, what is really created is "an outer appearance that is false self," which is used "to compensate for unrepaired damage." This is a subject where role reversal abounds, making much of what is bad look good and what is good and modest look bad. It is also an area where absurd extremes exist. Just because someone has a certain physical appearance does not necessarily mean they are compensating for shame or any other problem. However, the world is also full of extreme expressions of outer appearances, ones that are compensating for something internal. The point here is not to become a better judge of appearance, but it is to hold up a mirror.

We need to know if decisions relating to our own outer appearance are good decisions or bad ones that are compensating for internal problems. If shame is the motivator then no amount of changes to our appearance will heal what is inside. This It will simply hide the real issues in the fog and provide nothing in the way of protecting our hearts. We will become dependent on a false belief and create some of the most extreme codependency we can imagine. The more shame-based a person is, the more codependent they will become. An outer appearance that is based on generating lust will never bring satisfaction to the inside of a person. They are externally focused people in a constantly changing world, where personal identity is evasive. Enough will never be enough. Altering the physical appearance for the sole purpose of removing shame will not work either. It will bring temporary satisfaction but ultimately produce more shame, because what is in the fog is still alive. The real problem has not been identified, confronted, or defeated.

The good news is that hope is found through several sources. Recovery, Christianity, counseling, treatment, and other sources of healing are available. The next box on the diagram points to this principle: "Abused people have damaged protection. Recovery helps to repair the damage." It is one of the reasons that the 12-Step Recovery process works so well to help people who have become addicts and codependents. This process is what the Bible refers to as "sanctification," meaning to "clean up the inside." Codependents especially will believe that the right relationship will fix everything. This is why many codependents go through multiple relationships and marriages, searching for the right one to heal the wounds. The most codependent woman in the Bible had the same problem. Her story will be covered in Chapter Six.

Continuing clockwise around the diagram, the next box states "People with healthy Protection choose who has permission to access their Inner Heart." When healing comes by restoring a right relationship with God and other people, then we can make good decisions that are not shame-based. The more secure we are with our true identity in the "Inner Heart," the better we will be at making healthy decisions concerning people. No need for extremes, just a good balance of dependency that is rich in wisdom and void of toxic emotions. Achieving this condition takes time depending on the individual experience and willingness to change. They can only happen if we use the proper tools and work for them.

The most important factor to take away from this diagram is to understand *"there is something in the fog."* Something we cannot see but are running from. It is called shame, and it will cause us harm unless it is identified, confronted, and defeated.

Ron E. #8 is a man who has lived with a false sense of guilt most of his life. He has a son who has mental health problems but refuses to take his medication. The situation is like a roller coaster that never seems to level off, always in a rapid fall or quick rise. The son can function independently to a certain degree but cannot manage most of his own responsibilities. Ron E. #8 is a good man by all standards and has made every attempt to help with the issues, only to experience anger, frustration, and hostility from his son. The real problem for Ron E. #8 is his own fog. On one occasion he said he knew what he needed to do but was unable do it. In asking why, he said, "I am still obligated to the voice of my mother who said it was my job to take care of him." He went on to explain that, even though his Mom had since passed away, he still felt obligated to her statement. Something was in the fog.

Another common problem that exists in the fog is guilt. This subject can actually help us maintain a healthy lifestyle and is primarily used in the Bible to address the problem of sin. And since "*all have sinned and come short of the glory of God*," we are all guilty. Romans 3:10. Accepting our guilt as sinners is the key to salvation in Christ. We understand that our sin has offended God, and that Jesus paid the price on the cross for our guilt. "*An innocent person doesn't need a savior.*" James 2:10 says, "*Whoever keeps the whole law and yet stumbles in one point is guilty of breaking it all.*" Just being a good person is not good enough.

The challenge comes when guilt turns into an unhealthy emotion that leads to destructive behavior. We respond to guilt by becoming guiltier. A healthy sense of guilt before God will lead to sorrow and repentance. It motivates us to confess our sins and seek the Lord's forgiveness. He is faithful to forgive our guilt. "*If we claim to be without sin, we deceive ourselves and the truth is not in us. If we confess our sins, he is faithful and just and will forgive us our sins and purify us from all unrighteousness.*" I John 1:8-9.

To clean up from the inside we need a clear conscience. A sense of guilt is connected to our conscience, and this is where the real problem lies. A healthy conscience knows how to respond to guilt, a damaged one does not. Extreme criticism or rejection, abuse, divorce, or believing that you should be something else, anything but who you are, can lead to a wounded conscience.

Codependents in general have mastered the art of using unhealthy guilt statements, such as:

- "If you really loved me, then ...."
- "How can you call yourself a Christian?"
- "You made me feel guilty!"

These statements are based on guilt for the purpose of control and blame. The last statement is not even possible; no one can make another person feel anything. It is still our choice to decide, unless codependency has taken away those choices. The answer then becomes dealing with the guilt that is in the fog, not trying to project it onto other people and blame them. At the same time codependents will assume guilt for things they are not responsible for, such as someone else's bad decisions. Guilt for a codependent can also come from having to say "no," even when it is the right answer.

The opposite extreme for codependents with unhealthy guilt comes from trying to never be guilty; problems are always someone else's fault. A codependent Skunk will act this way, repelling others and blaming them, when it is the skunk who is the guilty one. Perfectionists will also have this issue, because never being guilty leaves no room to be human. Everyone make mistakes and some people can accept this fact, and others cannot.

One public demonstration of never being guilty can be observed in any professional basketball game. When the referee blows the whistle because a foul was committed, the most common response from the player is palms up, wrinkled face, look of disbelief. What is even funnier is when multiple players do the same thing for one whistle. Only one can be guilty, so why are the rest responding? It is easy to see this rejection of guilt as an automatic response, not based on any knowledge of truth, but it is simply a response ready at any time an accusation of guilt is presented. It is the same for codependents who have unhealthy guilt in the fog. They will automatically respond to an accusation with a rejection of guilt, and defend their position even when it is obvious they are wrong. This explains one of the healing aspects of codependency, which is to allow yourself to be human, make mistakes, and know that God and other people still love you. Healthy guilt is accepted by healthy people.

There is also the subject of false guilt. The difficulty comes for a codependent when all guilt is treated as false. A person with healthy dependency will be able to sort out true guilt from false guilt, which is the key to overcoming the destructive nature of this issue. To accomplish this one has to have to first take ownership of the guilty feelings, every last one of them. Avoiding a problem never solves it. Stay with the feeling; otherwise he/she will not know if it is true or false. If it is true guilt: confess, repent, and accept God's forgiveness, then correct any wrongs done, referred to in recovery as making amends. If it is false guilt, then how did it get through your protection? What part of you is unprotected from false guilt? This is where codependents get stuck with using their internal calculator, by claiming that others are "pushing their buttons." But that is not possible unless we provide access in the first place. The solution lies in embracing truth, repairing damage, and getting the false guilt out of the fog.

Another issue for codependents that hides in the fog is criticism. Just like guilt penetrates the inner heart of a person and causes damage, so can criticism. The typical response is to reject or run from any form of criticism, believing it provides protection from this issue. That is a fantasy, because there is no life on earth without criticism. Jesus was criticized and so was Moses, both by their own people. Why are we so surprised when criticism comes from sources that are close to us?

There are many examples of criticism that take place in the Bible. People criticized Jesus for not following the rules, and justified themselves because they did. Christians are often a target for criticism. If a person stands for what he/she believes in, then he/she will be criticized. If that same person does not stand for anything then he/she will be criticized. Either way people are going to be criticized. Just remember, Jesus never criticized sinners for acting like sinners, he just criticized religious people for acting like sinners. But if one really wants to be safe from criticism, don't do anything. Of course, that person will be criticized for doing nothing. There is no way to avoid criticism.

This subject exposes a unique codependent characteristic, those with the spiritual gift of criticism. They are living in the fog just like any other unhealthy codependent, but like to use the Bible as a license to criticize. There is an aspect of Scripture that confronts sin by pointing to truth. In the hands of a healthy person this can be used to bring people to God through compassion and understanding. In the hands of a codependent this will be used as a negative force. Their words, actions, and even public demonstration of Christianity will be saturated with criticism. They speak quickly, love company, justify self-actions, and find fault with what others are doing. Referring to this condition as being "in the fog" is an accurate and polite description. The truth is these people are abusive spiritually, emotionally, and mentally, and would benefit from codependency recovery.

"Those who consider themselves religious and yet do not keep a tight rein on their tongues deceive themselves, and their religion is worthless. Religion that God our Father accepts as pure and faultless is this: to look after orphans and widows in their distress and to keep oneself from being polluted by the world." James 1:26-27.

One evening I was walking with my family through a large city, and there were a lot of people out in public. We came upon two individuals holding large signs, proclaiming that God hated sin. From a short distance I stopped and watched the events unfold, as these two people screamed at people walking by, and other people screamed back in opposition. But what really caught my attention more than anything was the ineffective way that God was being presented, through dysfunctional criticism. The statement on the sign was true — God does hate sin — but the message is that He loved us so much that Jesus came to solve our guilt problem. The sign could have read "God loves sinners," and the two individuals could have raised their voices in proclaiming this truth. Criticism in the hands of a wise person produces positive results, but in the hands of a codependent it only produces a negative outcome.

As with other issues, there is a fine line between criticism that is healthy and unhealthy. There are good and bad forms of criticism. For someone who struggles with codependency it will be very hard to see the difference. If a person does not have good boundaries and still lives in the fog, then how are they going to discern between good and bad criticism? They will first have to identify the sources of their problems before they can be confronted and defeated.

A few extreme examples are never wanting to hear criticism and experiencing a flood of emotions when it happens. These are out-of-balance extremes that live in the fog. Another example is being unable to give healthy criticism, claiming to be a good person because you never criticize, which is just an excuse for not being able to give healthy criticism. The balance is found in being able to give and receive constructive criticism. The key is to know what the motive and purpose is. The purpose should be to build people up, not just tear them down. It should produce character and needs to be coupled with genuine respect and concern for the person who is receiving it. Codependents will generally be incapable of doing this until a transformation has taken place. They can only share what they have, and it is already toxic.

As with the subject of guilt, we need to develop the ability to hear criticism, or choose to accept it or reject it. Consider the source and the motive behind it. If it is not yours, then let it go; if it is yours then keep it, because it might help you to become a better person. In some cases you can ask a person if they are willing to hear some constructive criticism; just don't give unwanted advice free of charge. Codependents like to make "helpful" statements that are intended for the benefit of the other person, but have an agenda intended to make the other person do something. It sounds odd, but it actually helps us to listen to criticism and then choose what to do with it. Avoiding criticism is a false goal, no one can achieve it. Better to find out what is in the fog that cannot hear criticism and remove it.

Another example of all-or-nothing extremes that produces fog is parenting and protecting our children. We are responsible as parents to make every effort that is humanly possible to protect our children. When codependent fog creeps in, the issue of safety will go to a dysfunctional extreme. Parents will try to protect their children not only from harm but also from any discomfort in life.

They will try to make things easy on the kids so they do not have to struggle, or will defend anything their children do and blame everyone else for problems. Codependent statements will be made such as "the police need to do something" or "I cannot believe the way they run that school."

Many years ago while standing in a checkout line the grocery store, I was behind a cart that had a young child sitting in it who was about 4 years old. The mom and dad were just in front of the cart. I looked at the child, smiled and said hello. The child turned around and screamed to the parents, "Help, he is going to take me!" Quite frankly it was disgusting what the parents had done to protect their child. Of course, we need to teach them to be safe, but the level of fear they had placed in the child was extreme. The only thing they were creating was a neurotic kid who was sure to have emotional problems and not know how to trust safe people. It was, however, easy to see from watching mom and dad that they were in need of some emotional, mental, and perhaps spiritual healing. It appeared that the generational transfer of fog was taking place.

We have the opportunity to break the generational transfer of all these issues, or we can pass them on. Identifying the source of what is in the fog is not always necessary to confront it. Sometimes the fog needs to be cleared before we can see the origin, peeling the layers of the onion to expose what is underneath. Even if we do find the origin of the problem, that does not resolve the issue. If an alcoholic can figure out what makes him or her drink, does that produce sobriety? No. It is the same for codependents. Knowing how the fog began will not make it easier to understand, in fact it might produce blame and make it worse. Identifying what is in the fog is critical to confronting it, and ultimately defeating its influence.

There are many other subjects that could be listed and expanded upon as they relate to the fact that *"there is something in the fog."* The main idea is that codependency produces a condition in the mind and heart of a person that hides issues. As long as the codependency progresses, the issues will grow, multiply, and get worse. When changes are made to address the problems, clarity will come that will bring healing and inner freedom.

There is one lie to be aware of that will come out of the fog: change is too hard and will take too long. When a sincere and adequate effort is made to face the truth, it is only a short period of time before things start to change. During this time the situation may get worse before it gets better; in fact is almost a certainty. The idea that quitting a negative behavior will instantly produce a positive result is naïve. It is the part of us that wants a quick fix without effort. The truth is that other people are not going to respect our efforts to clear the fog and learn to set boundaries, especially if they are the ones who were violating them. Once a codependent starts setting boundaries they can expect the other person to double their efforts to get back to the old game. If the codependent caves in, it all starts over. But if they stand firm and don't compromise, the rewards will come. "*Stand firm then, with the belt of truth buckled around your waist,*" Ephesians 6:14.

In Exodus Chapter Five the Israelites are taking the first step towards freedom. Moses has returned from the desert and brought word to his people that God will deliver them from bondage in Egypt. He has met with all the leaders of Israel and told them what God is going to do. The problem has been identified; it is Pharaoh, and in God's power Moses is going to confront and defeat the problem. It must have been exciting for the Israelites; they had been in bondage all their lives. God's deliverance starts with Moses and Aaron going to Pharaoh and telling him to let the people go. Then the situation gets worse when the working conditions are made more difficult. God knew what He was doing, but the people did not. Even though the process of deliverance was starting, things got worse before they got better. The people had an expectation that deliverance would be easy, and they get angry when the problem was only confronted, not defeated.

Eventually Pharaoh is defeated after the ten plagues, and the Israelites leave Egypt. Not too long afterward their freedom is challenged when the enemy decides to go after them in the desert. The Israelites are backed up against the Red Sea, and the people tell Moses they want to quit and just go back to Egypt. Instead, Moses gives them instructions and God performs one of His greatest miracles, the parting of the Red Sea. The story ends with Israel safe and the enemy utterly defeated.

Nothing changes until the problem is identified, confronted, and defeated. During the process things will get worse before they get better. There will be frustration and discouragement, and it will be easier to quit and go back. But God has the path of deliverance already mapped out, and He will lead a person to freedom one step at a time. Rarely if ever does He give the whole plan up front. We simply need to trust in God, listen to others, and follow directions. Perfection is not necessary. We might get frustrated and complain, but we must not quit. Other people who have been part of the problem will pursue us with their agenda and issues; they will want us to return to our old ways. But we must stay the course because the journey will not last forever. That is a lie. Even though *"there is something in the fog,"* it will ultimately be defeated.

"Not only so, but we also glory in our sufferings, because we know that suffering produces perseverance; perseverance, character; and character, hope. And hope does not put us to shame, because God's love has been poured out into our hearts through the Holy Spirit, who has been given to us." Romans 5:3-5.

Are you ready for some secrets?

5

The Secret of Sin

" *When it comes to codependency, there are many secrets, and many sins.*" A common saying is that we "are only as sick as our secrets." Secret sin will keep you sick. I John 1:8-10 states, "*If we claim to be without sin, we deceive ourselves and the truth is not in us. If we confess our sins, he is faithful and just and will forgive us our sins and purify us from all unrighteousness. If we claim we have not sinned, we make him out to be a liar and his word is not in us.*" Codependency will make people believe they have insight into the secrets of others, all the while being blind to their own secrets and sins, thereby deceiving themselves. There are three key areas of codependency that follow this theme, leading many to confusion and denial.

The first is a belief that somehow exists all around the world, one that interprets struggles in life as God judging a person for their secret sin. This can be applied to an individual or a church. Some claim diseases fit into this category, or perhaps financial struggles, but it has been used on any subject that relates to difficulties in life. If a person is targeted with this type of accusation, and they claim to not understand what sin they are committing, they are labeled as liars because God is obviously judging them.

The main problem with this whole philosophy is that it relies on humans to interpret God's will. Not all churches believe this philosophy, but there are far too many that teach it as Biblical truth.

This belief is an abusive expression of codependency, because the people using it are falsely depending on external circumstances to interpret life. They see everything in all-or-nothing extremes; it is either no problems or all judgment. It is interesting though that the people doing the interpreting are not the ones struggling, they just claim to have some divine insight into the struggles of others. The Bible does have examples of people who properly interpreted life's circumstances, such as the Prophets of the Old Testament, but people need to study these examples closely before claiming to be on the same level. Israel had millions of people, but only a small number of prophets.

Dependence upon the Bible that produces a false doctrine happens when people believe they have wisdom when they do not. It is role reversal, by taking something good (the Bible) and using it for bad purposes, and taking something bad (false pride) and making it look good. How these types of belief systems get so ingrained into the church can seem hard to understand, but it is actually simple if we apply the principles of codependency. Externally-focused people in a constantly changing world, reversing the roles of good and bad, living in the extremes, abandoning what is right, and validating themselves in dysfunctional ways at the expense of others.

In the book of Acts Chapter 28 there is an example of this type of mindset. The apostle Paul is on a ship traveling to Rome when it runs aground and is destroyed. Everyone on board makes it ashore and encounters the local islanders, who show kindness by making a fire. Paul puts some wood on the fire and a snake jumps out and bites him. The response of the islanders is the same as Christians judging someone for secret sin. *"When the islanders saw the snake hanging from his hand, they said to each other, 'This man must be a murderer; for though he escaped from the sea, the goddess Justice has not allowed him to live.' But Paul shook the snake off into the fire and suffered no ill effects. The people expected him to swell up or suddenly fall dead; but after waiting a long time and seeing nothing unusual happen to him, they changed their minds and said he was a god."* Acts 28:4-6.

Both of these interpretations were wrong. The islanders were familiar enough with their immediate surroundings to recognize the snake as lethal. But their ability to properly interpret the situation was tainted by a lack of wisdom into the will of God. They did not understand the person, the circumstances, or the purpose of either. Yet they quickly jumped to a false conclusion based only on what they could see and on what appeared to be a sign.

The Pharisees that Jesus spoke with had the same problem. *"Then some of the Pharisees and teachers of the law said to him, 'Teacher, we want to see a sign from you.' He answered, 'A wicked and adulterous generation asks for a sign!'"* Matthew 12:38-39. Evidently looking for a sign to interpret the mind of God is not a good practice. Instead of leading people towards God, it actually takes them away from Him where they are only depending on themselves for divine insight. The result is a conclusion that is void of God's wisdom, a contradiction at its core. People who are only familiar with their own surroundings try to judge issues without understanding the people, the circumstances, or God's purpose.

I was first exposed to this idea of God judging for secret sin during a trip to Russia, while talking with a woman who was asking for help with her own codependency. As the translator interpreted it became clear that this woman was suffering emotionally and spiritually. She told of her daughter becoming sick and dying at the age of 12. The illness lasted for three years, during which time she took her daughter to doctors and clergy. She had literally tried anything she could to find a cure. During that time a minister told her that the daughter was sick because God was judging the secret sin of this mother. A doctor who was unable to diagnose the illness said the child was suffering from a lack of love. After the child died, this woman continued for years to search for the sin that had caused her daughter's death. She looked me dead in the eye and through the interpreter said, "I still don't know what I did." Part of my response was to tell her that she had been lied to. Both the clergy and doctor were falsely depending on a lack of insight to interpret the situation, and both were wrong. The minister did not understand her, the circumstances, or God's purpose for either, but somehow felt qualified to speak on God's behalf.

This belief has raised its ugly head all over the world within Christian circles. Not for all churches or followers of Christ, but too many use it as a way of discerning someone else's struggles. If this belief is false then the Bible will clearly show it, and in fact it does. From the beginning in Genesis to the end of Revelation the Bible refutes this false belief. To properly apply God's judgment of sin we need to understand an undeniable truth, that *"God reveals sin before He judges it."* From the Garden of Eden in Genesis to the judgment seat of Christ in Revelation, God judges the sins of mankind "after" he reveals it. The following are just a few examples:

- Genesis Chapter 3. The first sin.

   After Adam and Eve sinned, God questioned them about why they were hiding and who had told them they were naked. The attention is then focused on the serpent, whom God questions as well. The entire situation is discussed in verses 8-13 before any action is taken. Afterward verse 14 states: *"So the LORD God said to the serpent, "Because you have done this,…"*, and then passed down the judgment. The serpent's consequences came after the sin was revealed. Adam and Eve also receive consequences, "after" their sin was revealed.

- II Samuel Chapter 12. The King of Israel.

   The prophet Nathan goes to confront King David about his adultery with Bathsheba and his scheme to hide it which resulted in the death of her husband Uriah. Nathan tells a story as if it were about someone else, then in verse 7 reveals the sin of the King by saying to David, *"You are the man!"* In verse 14 Nathan tells David, *"But because by doing this you have shown utter contempt for the LORD, the son born to you will die."*

The judgment upon David is the death of the child which was conceived in sin with Bathsheba. Nathan tells David about the consequences "after" the sin was revealed. Later on when the child died, David did not wonder what secret sin he had committed; he already knew. This story follows a principle that God established: sin is revealed before it is judged.

- Acts Chapter 5. The story of Ananias and Sapphira.

These two entrepreneurs sold a piece of land and tried to fool Peter into believing they had given all the proceeds to the church. The truth is they secretly held back some of the money for themselves — truly a secret sin. God was so displeased with their deception that it cost them their lives, "after" it was revealed.

Peter said to Ananias in verses 4-5: *"'What made you think of doing such a thing? You have not lied just to human beings but to God.' When Ananias heard this, he fell down and died."* Sapphira arrives at the temple without knowing their scheme had been exposed. She had the chance to tell the truth, but continued lying instead. Peter then said to her in verse 9-10: *"How could you conspire to test the Spirit of the Lord? Listen! The feet of the men who buried your husband are at the door, and they will carry you out also.' At that moment she fell down at his feet and died."*

Both had agreed to lie about the money, and God revealed this through Peter before giving them the consequences. The principle of God revealing sin before He judges it occurs twice in this story. This was truly a sin of secrecy, yet God still chose to reveal the secret first and judge it afterward. It also shows that if God grants divine wisdom into the sin of another person, then the nature of the sin is known by the person who is interpreting. There is no guessing or lack of knowledge, no secrets, because the specifics are known to both parties. The person who speaks about judgment for secret sin knows the details of the people, the circumstances, and God's purpose, as was the case with Nathan and King David.

- Revelation Chapter 20. The Great White Throne.

This is recorded as an event taking place apart from this earth, after a person physically dies. Verse 12 states: *"And I saw the dead, great and small, standing before the throne, and books were opened. Another book was opened, which is the book of life. The dead were judged according to what they had done as recorded in the books."* The principle of God revealing sin before He judges it extends even beyond this earth. It is an eternal principle that is clearly shown throughout the Bible.

There is only one story in the Bible that could be used to support the belief that difficulties in life are a result of God judging for secret sin. It is found in the Book of Joshua where Israel is defeated in a battle for no reason. They had multiple successes in battle before, but are suddenly defeated. Joshua comes before the Lord and is told that the sin will be revealed the next day, that someone in the camp has spoils from a previous battle which they were told not to take. This scripture is also used by Christians to state that "there is sin in the camp," presenting the idea that struggles by a church or Christian organization are a result of God judging the whole group for the secret sin of a few people. This is just another way of believing that something secretive is going on, and the only way anyone knows is because of struggles that no one can explain, so it must be secret sin.

While the application of this scripture is one of God judging a secret that others were not aware of, it also shows God revealing where the sin existed before bringing individual judgment. In Joshua 7:14, the process is described ahead of time: "*In the morning, present yourselves tribe by tribe. The tribe the* LORD *chooses shall come forward clan by clan; the clan the* LORD *chooses shall come forward family by family; and the family the* LORD *chooses shall come forward man by man. Whoever is caught with the devoted things shall be destroyed by fire.*" The next morning Joshua follows the Lord's instructions, and through this process the guilty party is revealed as Achan. Then judgment comes upon him and his family, "after" the sin was revealed.

So how do churches all over the world arrive at a false belief based on one scripture? Actually it is just half a scripture, because the second half supports the principle of someone understanding the sin they are being judged for. So, does this half scripture then support the idea that struggles in life are a result of God judging someone for secret sin? No, not without them understanding what sin they committed before being judged. The conclusion is that if a person is struggling and they do not know what they have done, and then it is "not" God's judgment. The only correct conclusion from this scripture in Joshua is that God will judge a nation for the sins of individuals even if they are done in secret. He will also judge the individual for the same sin, after revealing it.

Christians use this philosophy as a codependent form of pride. It sounds real intelligent if someone can sit back and claim to have special insight into the mind of God, claiming they know something that others do not. In other words, they are externally-focused people, taking what is bad (themselves) and trying to make it look good, and taking what is good (God) and making it look bad. Those who use this false principle can cause pain, suffering, and consequences in the lives of other people. The focus is really on themselves, trying to look wise and discerning when they are not. The whole idea places dependence on a person to play the role of God in someone else's life, a common characteristic of codependency. The end result is harm to other people, such as the mother in Russia suffering under the false guilt of somehow causing her daughter's death.

At times God does give people wisdom into the sins of others, such as Peter with Ananias and Sapphira. It is wisdom with proper dependence upon God, one that is a balance of human understanding and God's knowledge. People who state that others are being judged for secret sin without knowing what that sin is are codependent humans who are out of balance with God's wisdom. Otherwise, according to the examples in Scripture, they would have specific insight into the nature of the sin, such as the Prophet Nathan with David.

That is the test. If a person tries to claim that someone else is being judged for secret sin but does not know what the sin is, then they are what the Bible calls a "false prophet," and there are warnings in the scriptures about this type of person. *"Watch out for false prophets. They come to you in sheep's clothing, but inwardly they are ferocious wolves. By their fruit you will recognize them."* Matthew 7:15-16. If they cannot produce the fruit of knowledge of the sin that they claim is being judged, then inwardly they are void of truth and have no idea what they are talking about. It is also proof that God is absent from the wisdom they claim to possess; they're just wolves pretending to be sheep.

There is another form of false knowledge that closely relates to the belief of judgment for secret sin. It has to do with God not removing struggles in life because of lack of faith on our part. One personal example was a Christian man who told me that people who die of diseases do so because of a personal lack of faith, claiming that the Bible clearly stated this as truth. He also said this just a few months after my Mom had died of cancer. I asked him to clarify what I had just heard, and he pretty much repeated the same thing. We had some discussion that was not very pleasant, especially since he knew what had happened and chose to say this anyway. Not surprisingly this man showed severe symptoms of codependency in several other areas of his life. There seems to be a very strong connection between people who readily pick up false beliefs and those who are codependent. I would not describe these people as wise or discerning, more like deceived and delusional. The element of pride is consistent with those who claim both the secret sin and lack of faith insights. They seem very proud of themselves for being wise, yet fail to see the increase in pain they are causing in the lives of others, and the contradiction they are making to Scripture. They also fail to see the true secret, their own codependency. Secret sin will keep you sick, especially when it is your own.

Moving on to another form of sin related to codependency, the subject of "offence." People in general are easily offended, and most often believe they are entitled to something based on their offence, but not according to the Bible. The connection of offence to codependency is common in the basic elements that are revealed in a variety of ways. For example, an externally-focused person can be easily offended by others not agreeing with their extreme agenda, and try to express it through role reversal to make others look bad for disagreeing. The codependency is expressed through aggressive hostility, which is why The Environmentalist from Chapter Two is defined as a "flaming" codependent. Offended codependents are like a fireball rolling their way through life. They hurt other people and feel justified because of their own offended attitudes. The subject of people being offended and entitled is an issue of codependency since others are supposed to cave in or walk on eggshells as not to upset them. Otherwise people will face the retribution of their anger, just like a codependent in a family who controls people with rage.

In the movie "Forrest Gump" there is a series of events that are set at the nation's capital. Forrest and his lifelong girl, Jenny, have been reunited and are spending some time together. But there is a boyfriend involved who is traveling with Jenny, one who hits her and is subsequently attacked by Forrest. The next day, Jenny needs to get on the bus to leave and the boyfriend shows up to make things right. He apologizes, but quickly identifies the source of his problems as that "lying Johnson," blaming the U.S. President for his actions. The reasoning seems to be that the boyfriend is so offended by the "lying Johnson" that he cannot control his actions, and blames being offended for his violent behavior. All offended codependents have a "lying Johnson" story, because they need it to justify being offended, as well as making excuses for their actions.

"The negative voice is always loud." It has to be heard, at least from the perspective of the negative person. People are offended by politics claiming that it is because of that "lying Johnson", or whoever they substitute. The truth is they were predisposed to extreme reactions before that "lying Johnson" ever got elected, and the elected official just became a reason to blame their offended attitudes and sometimes violent behavior. People need it to justify the expressions of their own internal conflict. In fact, they depend on it. When a whole community erupts in violence over an incident involving one person, are we to believe all of those out of control were at peace until the incident happened? Of course not, but the message is that the expression of emotions were caused by the incident, because they were offended.

There is no difference between these types of events and the codependent expressing their own out of control emotions on their family or co-workers, then using their "lying Johnson" reason to justify it. It is not always politics; it could be anything where the excuse for being offended has nothing to do with the current problem. In these circumstances, people are expressing their own codependency problems, by blaming the external world for why they are so easily offended. Codependents will challenge this truth by playing the victim role and claiming that protesting has nothing to do with codependency, so they are victims of a false label. But when they are blaming a decision or event in society to justify their own out of control emotions and behavior, then they are depending on it as an excuse for their own pre-existing internal problems, which is codependency.

Here are two examples:
"Oh, so you're saying that people who protest are all just codependents?"
"No, I'm saying that if you blame an incident for your own out-of-control emotions and behavior, then you are depending on it as an excuse, which is codependency."

"The codependent is predisposed to reacting." A mild codependent will have more subtle expressions of being offended, while the flaming codependent will be more like a ball of fire launched from a catapult. Whomever they contact will suffer the impact. The passive codependent is no less destructive; they have just mastered the art of calmly reacting to being offended, and will look for ways to control other people through influence. The courts of law are busy with this type of codependent, since there is no need to get out of control when changing the law forces everyone to comply. *"Being offended has become a false cure for codependency."* But it is a contradiction to heal internally from the pains of life and continue to be easily offended. One is the solution, the other is the problem.

One of the first times I had the opportunity to "preach" at a Sunday morning worship service, controversy showed up. When one family, members of the church, found out who was preaching, they walked out and quit the church in protest. The excuse was given that a man who has been divorced should not be allowed to preach. The family was so offended that apparently leaving and quitting the church was the only option they had. The truth is this family had a history of church membership that was a revolving door. Every time something did not go their way they quit, and later came back. It was always that "lying Johnson," pointing at something to blame for their offended attitudes and to justify their behavior. My personal observation leaned towards a hyper-spiritual family, one that was predisposed to making grand public expressions of being offended. As far as I know, there were no addictions in this family, but codependency ran strong through the family tree.

This points to one of the common codependent traits of an easily offended person: an external appearance of super spirituality. This condition is used to compensate for what is lacking on the inside. Some Christians or churches claim to live by a "high standard," which is portrayed as an uncompromising life of extreme discipline. These people seem to be the same ones that are easily offended, highly critical, and claim that struggles in life are judgments from God for secret sin. Genuine spirituality is an outward expression of what is already genuine on the inside. It reveals a heart that is at peace with God and cares about hurting people, and a mind that thinks about others before self. It is not surprising that people who demonstrate genuine spirituality in their attitudes and actions are not easily offended.

There are a lot of scriptures from both the Old and New Testaments about the subject of offence. Some are just a single verse, and others are whole stories. They provide valuable insight into understanding how we should respond and warnings about the pitfalls of being offended for the wrong reasons.

One conclusion we can stand on: offence is not an attribute to be desired. We will be offended at some point; what we do when offended will determine the impact on our character. If we allow it to become ingrained into our hearts and minds, then it will have a negative impact on our attitudes, words, and actions. If we use it as opportunity for growth, then we will be more like Jesus. He had every reason to be offended, more than we ever will. Instead, He told parables and responded in ways that gave us examples to follow.

Four Bible Stories Relating to Offense.

- Luke 15:25-32. The Prodigal Son.

   The story of the Prodigal son is a familiar one, even to people who do not regularly read the Bible. The main plot of the story is about a young man who leaves home, makes a lot of bad decisions, but is welcomed back with loving arms by his father. The story is a picture of our Heavenly Father loving us unconditionally, no matter what we have done to offend Him.

A lesson on offence comes from another character in this story, the prodigal son's brother. His part of the story is short and comes at the end. The father of both sons is celebrating the prodigal's return by having a feast, and *"the older brother became angry and refused to go in. So his father went out and pleaded with him. But he answered his father, 'Look! All these years I've been slaving for you and never disobeyed your orders. Yet you never gave me even a young goat so I could celebrate with my friends.'"* Luke 15:28-29.

"Offence will take away your ability to rejoice in someone else's blessings."

When people are offended the attention is being drawn toward themselves. It is really not about the circumstances or other people involved, it is "all about me." This state of being offended is an expression of preexisting codependency. In this story the brother is basically saying, "Look at all I did for you, and this is the thanks I get." He has no interest in the good that is taking place and only wants to turn it into something bad. The brother is actually trying to convince the father that his offended attitude is worth listening to. Have you ever complained to God about someone else being blessed? Maybe not directly in prayer, but at least in thought, especially when the other person gets something you really wanted.

Codependents will find it difficult to rejoice in other people's blessings. Outwardly they might smile and say the right words, but inwardly they will be offended. If another church is growing but not yours, a codependent minister or member will struggle to rejoice for the other church. Even though it means people are connecting with God and finding hope, offence will take away the ability to rejoice in someone else's blessing. One of the measures of our own spirituality is when we see someone else get the blessing we desired, and we are genuinely happy for them. Otherwise we are like the prodigal son's brother, who missed the celebration because of being offended.

- Jonah 3:10-4:5. Jonah is sent to Nineveh.

The story of Jonah is proof that God can use dysfunctional people to do incredible things. He is called by God to go to Nineveh and preach repentance, since the city has fallen into deep sin. Instead, he decides to go sailing out in the ocean the opposite way. God needs him to go to Nineveh so He creates circumstances that lead Jonah to dry land and back on his path. After the city accepts his message and repents of its sins, Jonah throws a pity party. He goes up on the hill and complains to God, because he is offended. *"Jonah had gone out and sat down at a place east of the city. There he made himself a shelter, sat in its shade and waited to see what would happen to the city."* Jonah 4:5. Not only did his offence take away his ability to rejoice in someone else's blessing, it caused another condition.

"Offence will lead you to despair, isolation, and self-pity."

Jonah had a discussion with God where he expressed his displeasure with the outcome. In this dialogue we see his attitude, revealed by going outside the city by himself and complaining. In fact, at one point Jonah asked God to just take his life, a sign of extreme despair. While there are many lessons to learn from this short book of the Bible, we can surely see what happens to a person that becomes offended, even when the circumstances are about someone or something else. This whole story is really about the people of Nineveh, of God showing mercy and forgiveness for repentance. But when Jonah attached a good outcome to his bad attitude, he claims to be offended. The truth is he was ready to be offended before he ever left for the journey, which is why he tried to go somewhere else. Jonah had a preexisting condition in his heart and mind.

Saying that offence will never lead to anything good is an understatement. In the hands of codependent, offence is like a lethal weapon. In fact, the physical toll that codependent offence takes on a person is lethal. Codependency can take life away from a person slowly and painfully, through stress, lack of sleep, and poor physical health. These people will wake you up in the middle of the night with a crisis that cannot wait until morning. Since they are in turmoil, others need to join in as well. People will eventually make every effort to get away from this type of person. It is a lifestyle that will lead to despair, isolation, and self-pity.

- I Kings Chapter 21. Jezebel.

What a picture that name conjures up. Not exactly one of character and beauty, more like someone to deliberately avoid. Among the many sins of Jezebel was being offended when her husband had a problem. She apparently thought it was her responsibility to take up an offence that was not hers. Her husband Ahab was wallowing in pity, because he wanted a vineyard that the owner would not sell to him. Jezebel sees him sulking and inquires as to the problem. She decides to take up her husband's offence, and on his behalf does things that are evil by nature. *"His wife Jezebel came in and asked him, 'Why are you so sullen? Why won't you eat?' He answered her, 'Because I said to Naboth the Jezreelite, 'Sell me your vineyard; or if you prefer, I will give you another vineyard in its place.' But he said, 'I will not give you my vineyard.'" Jezebel his wife said, 'Is this how you act as king over Israel? Get up and eat! Cheer up. I'll get you the vineyard of Naboth the Jezreelite.'"* I Kings 21:5-7.

Jezebel then plots to produce false witnesses and accusations against Naboth, and as a result he is stoned to death. The Prophet Elisha goes to Ahab and warns him, *"And also concerning Jezebel the LORD says: 'Dogs will devour Jezebel by the wall of Jezreel.'* I

Kings 21:23. This is another example of God revealing sin before He judges it, and giving specific insight to the person who is exposing the sin. It also points to a principle relating to offence: *"Taking up another person's offence will lead to problems in your own life."*

We see this throughout our world today. If an offence has occurred to another person or group of people, those with codependency will attach themselves to the offence. Even though the situation has nothing to do with them, it can be used to fuel aggressive behavior and blame something else. It can also be an excuse for deep-seated negative emotions and attitudes. Getting angry about real or perceived injustices done to others is simply an act of codependency. Quite often the offence had nothing to do with the offended. Even when there is a direct link based on ethnic background or cultural history, being offended is the only alternative and the solution involves gaining something externally such as money, land, or control. People believe that healing from the past can come from acquisition of land or gaining rights, a false dependency that is really codependency.

When this issue of taking up another person's offence is brought to the attention of a codependent, they will defend themselves by shifting attention to some rhetorical question. It is the "Whac-A-Mole" codependent. Anytime the conversation gets close to a common sense challenge to their agenda, they quickly shift the conversation in another direction. Role reversal is a common tactic when trying to make anyone look bad who does not agree. This is another example where codependents will play the victim role. They claim that being offended by injustices to other people has nothing to do with codependency, so they are just victims of a false label. But when they use those injustices as a reason to justify their out-of-control hostility, they are depending on it as an excuse for their own preexisting internal problem, codependency.

Here are two examples:
"Oh, so you're saying that if I am offended by injustices to other people that I'm a codependent?"
"No, I'm saying that if you use those injustices as a reason to vent hostility, then it's just an excuse for your own preexisting codependency."

Taking a stand against something that is wrong is not a problem. In fact, history is full of people who reached beyond their own influence to help others. The difference is found in what the true motive is. Servants will help when there is nothing to gain; codependents will help for selfish purposes to gain something. Perhaps the best way to understand this principle is to apply the picture from the Introduction of justice being represented by a set of scales in balance. It was stated that dependency implies a balance that works where one side can exceed the other to a degree and still be in balance; otherwise the scales become out of balance and unable to function properly. *Codependency occurs anytime dependence exceeds the limits that God has established.*

At certain times we do need to "carry each other's burdens," but even those situations demand proper balance to avoid codependency. People who take up another person's offence for the purpose of expressing their own codependency will create problems in their own lives. God wants us to help people by serving Him, not take over the situation and try to control it through our own influence. It is very difficult for certain codependents to understand this because they are so emotionally attached to the offence that letting go is unthinkable. One of the most common tools of codependent recovery is to "let go, and let God," which applies to taking up another person's offence. We need to have clear honesty when supporting a cause to avoid taking up someone else's offence simply as an excuse for our own codependency.

- Matthew Chapter 13. The people of Jesus' hometown.

    During Jesus' ministry He went to a synagogue in His home-
town. There He taught them from the Scriptures, and instead of
accepting the message they questioned the messenger. Claiming they knew Jesus because He was from that area, they were
offended by His teaching. Can you imagine that they were in the
presence of Jesus Himself, and rejected Him because they were
offended over a ridiculous reason? "*Coming to his hometown,
he began teaching the people in their synagogue, and they were
amazed. 'Where did this man get this wisdom and these mirac-
ulous powers?' they asked. 'Isn't this the carpenter's son? Isn't
his mother's name Mary, and aren't his brothers James, Joseph,
Simon and Judas? Aren't all his sisters with us? Where then did
this man get all these things?' And they took offense at him.*"
Matthew 13:54-58.
    "*Being offended will lead you to reject the wrong people.*"
    One of the most codependent activities in churches is being
offended, by anything. It goes so far that there must be an undoc-
umented spiritual gift of "criticism." Offended by the music, the
message, the way some people dress, or talk, or look. The list
is exhaustive and so is the subject. Ask any church what their
mission is, and it will tie somehow to reaching and loving people
for God. People who are then offended by those they reach will
eventually reject the wrong people, the ones who need Jesus.
    An evangelist came to our church one Sunday and preached
a message that I will never forget. He talked about fishing for
bass and catching blowfish and carp instead, and commented
how the fisherman probably wished they hadn't caught those
ones. The point was made that when we follow the commandments of Christ to fish for men, we will catch ones that are not
always the kind we were hoping for. When Jesus called some of
the disciples to follow Him, they were told they would be fishers
of men, but they were never told what kind they would catch.

If the church is trying to reach people for Christ, then people need to realize that some are going to be unpleasant. Being offended by difficult people will lead you to reject the wrong people. Hurting people already know what it feels like to be hurt; what they need to know is what it feels like to be loved. That is the example Jesus gave us, and it requires the absence of offence. Codependents have trouble with this aspect of Christianity; they are stuck in predictable pattern of false dependency. When difficult people show up they get offended. "Wish we hadn't caught that one" would be an honest answer, but it usually comes out in criticism or wanting to change that person to fit a familiar mold. The change God is looking for takes place on the inside; codependents are looking on the outside. A church music director once said that a long-term member told him to quit tapping his foot while singing. He was signing praises from his heart to the God of heaven, and apparently God does not like foot tapping. Being offended will lead you to reject the wrong people.

The following are a few other scriptures relating to Offence:

- Proverbs 29:22. *"Offence will lead you to commit many sins."*

  "An angry person stirs up conflict, and a hot-tempered person commits many sins."

- Proverbs 18:19. *"People who are offended are difficult to communicate with."*

  "An offended friend is harder to win back than a fortified city. Arguments separate friends like a gate locked with bars." (NLT)

- Psalm 59:2-4. *"The Lord will defend us against false accusers, no offence needed."*

  "Deliver me from evildoers and save me from those who are after my blood. See how they lie in wait for me! Fierce men conspire

against me for no offense or sin of mine, Lord. I have done no wrong, yet they are ready to attack me. Arise to help me; look on my plight!"

It is obvious that being offended will lead to problems, and since codependency is so closely related to the subject of offense there needs to be methods of resolving these issues. The Bible has solid directions for responding to being offended.

- Proverbs 17:9. Cover the offence.

"Whoever would foster love covers over an offense, but whoever repeats the matter separates close friends."

"Let go" of the offence instead of bringing up the issue repeatedly. This applies to the common recovery phrase to "let go and let God." A person who "repeats matters" is someone who uses the past like dirty ashes from a fireplace. They cannot let go of past and have to keep throwing it at you, to make sure the messy details are remembered. Everyone is offended at some point in his or her life, and since we spend most of our time with those who are closest to us, they are the most likely ones to offend.

The principle here is that love will cover an offence. If it was a painful situation it will be harder to address, and pretending like it never happened will only make matters worse. Facing the issue and choosing to love the person more than repeating the matter will cover the offence. It means you don't have to talk about it constantly, but if it serves any good purpose it can be uncovered and then covered again. We have all witnessed this at some point, where people who have healed from an offence can talk about it at the right time and for the right purpose. Sharing about past pains can help others to find healing and grow spiritually. It is the power of our testimony, and God can use it to bless others if we have learned how to cover the offence with love. However, when someone uncovers the offence as a means of gossiping or judging, then harm will come to the relationship.

Codependents find it very difficult to cover an offence. They are too attached and still using it as an excuse for bitterness or some other negative aspect of life. A person cannot cover the offence and continue to depend on it as an excuse at the same time. Healthy dependence will allow a person to cover the offence, and occasionally uncover it for a constructive purpose. Codependency will cause a person who tries to uncover the offense to use it for harm. Until changes are made on the inside it will be impossible to express them on the outside.

- Proverbs 19:1. Overlook the offence.

"A person's wisdom yields patience; it is to one's glory to overlook an offense."

Being patient with others builds character. There are some offences that are less intense than others. These can happen at work or perhaps while doing something in public like shopping or dining in a restaurant. Someone says or does something that offends us; what we do with it is up to us. It helps to separate those things that are deliberate from the ones that are unintentional. Codependents will have a hard time with this; their self-focus will make everything seem intentional. The truth is a lot of the things we are offended by were not deliberate. It takes wisdom to have a positive outlook with people and make "unintentional" your first choice. Then we will have the ability to overlook the offence, and according to this scripture "it is to one's glory" to do so. If that is true, then how much more when the offence was deliberate and we choose to overlook it anyway. The bottom line is we have a choice, and if wisdom can prevail then we find solutions that bring healing. People who are not acting for God's glory remain offended.

One area where this plays out is in programs that help people with addictions and codependency. Recovery programs are just like churches. They are designed as a place where the more experienced people are there to help the new people. When people first arrive at recovery programs they are often not pleasant to deal with. They are hurting, suffering, and feeling lots of pain. They will do and say things that are offensive. Wisdom will yield patience and the ability to overlook the offence. It is a dynamic of recovery programs that makes them strong in helping difficult people. Find a church that has the same dynamic and you will find a diverse group who knows how to love difficult people and overlook offences.

One other thing to keep in mind about intentional vs. unintentional offences: we are guilty of both. Offence can simply be based on not understanding what someone was saying. One principle that can help to overlook an offence is to respond instead of reacting. This is another tool of recovery primarily taught in codependency groups. Reacting to an offense will make it difficult to overlook, responding will make it possible. A response can be anything that does not increase the problem.

- Matthew 6:12-15. Forgiveness.

"And forgive us our debts, as we also have forgiven our debtors."
We ask God to forgive us as we forgive others. The ultimate solution to being offended is to forgive. Sometimes this is easy and other times it is the most difficult thing to do, but in both situations it is the right answer. This is where people who take up the offence of another will be challenged. So much emotion and pride go into taking up another person's offence that forgiveness is not an option. It is impossible to do both, to forgive and keep the offence. Making the right decision with offence is based on principles, not emotions. We may not feel like doing what is right but we can do it anyway. Even if we have the right emotions it needs to be combined with the right principles to succeed. Reaching the point of forgiveness takes the right principles first, followed by the right emotions, which will eventually lead to the right actions.

Having a conversation with someone we were offended by should take place after we forgive them. Trying to resolve the situation without forgiving first will fail, because the problem is being brought into the solution. Resolving conflict with others is the end result of a process that includes forgiveness. Trying to short circuit the process for quick results will turn into more problems. Sometimes we forgive for no other reason than acknowledging how much God has forgiven us, and it works.

- Romans 12:20-21. Prayer & Gifts.

"'If your enemy is hungry, feed him; if he is thirsty, give him something to drink. In doing this, you will heap burning coals on his head.' Do not be overcome by evil, but overcome evil with good."

For a codependent this might seem like a desirable scripture, especially the part about heaping burning coals on their head. This reads like two good ideas with a bad one in the middle, but it is a complete process of right attitudes that will lead to right actions.

Take the first two statements. It says "enemy," someone with whom there is an intense problem. The resolve is to give your enemy a gift that will get their attention. That is what the burning coals analogy means. It is not a suggestion to cause pain for your enemy, but if you did put a burning coal in their head it would get their attention immediately. Acts of kindness to an enemy will get attention too. If we are not overcome by evil, but are determined to overcome evil with good, then it will get our enemy's attention. In fact, they probably will not be an enemy afterward. *"A gift to an offender will get their attention."*

One of the simple and practical suggestions for resolving an offence is to pray for God to bless that person with everything He has given you and more. This may not be as literal as giving them a tangible gift, but if we believe God answers prayers then perhaps we are giving something better than material items. Sincerely praying this way will do at least one thing; it will change our attitudes towards that person.

For the more difficult situations it is suggested that we do this every day for two weeks. At first it may be mechanical and not well intended. The best we can do might be: "God, please give them everything they deserve." But if we persist with an honest desire, it will wear down the offended attitudes and we will eventually realize that God gave us gifts that we did not deserve. Why would we not want others to have the same? The only thing that would truly keep us from such a desire is codependency. As long as we hold on to the right to be right, the need to be offended, our "lying Johnson" agendas, or the focus on external problems, we will not overcome evil with good. We will however be overcome by evil and never find peace. "*Remembering the words the Lord Jesus himself said: 'It is more blessed to give than to receive.'*" Acts 20:35.

The secret of the sin of offence is that it provides its own punishment. As long as a person remains offended they will continue to pay a price for it. There are consequences for holding onto an offence when we need to cover it, overlook it, and forgive. We cannot violate a scriptural principle and get a blessing. The Bible has clear directions on dealing with offence as an attitude. The principles of offence explain why codependency can be more destructive than addiction. Unresolved codependency can destroy good people, ruin families, and cause immeasurable damage to relationships, including ours with God. People who want to remain offended will deny this truth, but that doesn't change the truth. Justifying sin never leads to peace. Applying Biblical solutions will produce the right results.

The third subject to cover regarding the secret of sin is "judging." Proper dependence on God's principles will create an understanding of the subject of judging, one that is within the balance of the scales God has established. However, an out-of-balance extreme will be created when we make the same mistake as Adam and Eve, by accepting information that redefines truth. This subject has lead many people into extremes that contradict Scripture, while at the same time using Scripture as the source of information to prove their point. As with other subjects in this book, the principle of judging is a broad subject that goes far beyond the topic of codependency. It is, however a subject, that has an impact on codependents, so it will be covered to that extent.

It is common to hear people say, "I don't judge." This gives an appearance of wisdom and open mindedness as something to be desired. But is it as good as it sounds? Quite frankly, no. Even the people who claim not to judge will judge others who do not agree with them. There is also a statement that says, "I don't judge no one, and no one judges me." It is not even good English, and again we have an appearance of wisdom that is saturated in false beliefs. Would a person who uses these statements want them to be used in a court of law? They probably would want the judge to use wisdom and discernment, not just sit there and say, "I don't judge no one, and no one judges me."

People who use these statements are practicing a form of codependency. We are supposed to judge between right and wrong, good and evil, etc. The apostle Paul judged the Corinthians in Chapter Five of his first letter. He said, "*I have already passed judgment*" against one who was sinning openly. Do we not teach our children to judge character so they remain safe? Would we tell them "don't judge people" just because they look evil? Of course not. "I don't judge" is an excuse for not taking responsibility to call what is wrong as being wrong. In other words, it is an easy way out of discerning the choices between good and evil. It is role reversal, giving the appearance of wisdom while having none. "*Study to shew thyself approved unto God, a workman that needeth not to be ashamed, rightly dividing the word of truth.*" II Timothy 2:15 (KJV).

To understand how judging relates to codependency we have to recognize what it looks like. If codependents are externally focused people in a constantly changing world, then judging those things that are outside is mandatory. It is not even an option; a codependent has to judge the world. As the externals change so does the codependent's opinion of them. Role reversal demands judgment to make what is good look bad and what is bad look good. Codependents do not easily accept themselves as being part of the problem, but are quick to identify others as the source of trouble. Running to extremes is the result of judging with codependent eyes. The problem is not judging, the problem is doing so with the spiritual, emotional, and mental problems of codependency. Correct the problem and you will have the ability to exercise Godly judgment. This issue ties back to the problem of the fog. "*When it comes to the subject of judging, there is something in the fog of codependency.*"

In the Sermon on the Mount Jesus gave some instructions in which he specifically said, "*Do not judge.*" Matthew 7:1. People like to park right there and ignore other scriptures, using this statement to justify not judging. But an interesting contrast is made in I Corinthians 6:2-3, which states, "*Or do you not know that the Lord's people will judge the world? And if you are to judge the world, are you not competent to judge trivial cases? Do you not know that we will judge angels? How much more the things of this life!*" When the Bible appears to have a contradiction then we need to gain more understanding; Scripture never contradicts itself. The answer is found in learning that all uses of the word "judging" in the Bible do not have the same meaning. This is where judging secret sins in the lives of other people is a problem, by using the wrong scripture for the wrong application.

The first thing to understand is that judging is part of God's character. "*For we will all stand before God's judgment seat.*" Romans 14:10. Yet even with this impending day we don't have to fear, because another scripture tells us that "*God is love. Whoever lives in love lives in God, and God in them. This is how love is made complete among us so that we will have confidence on the Day of Judgment.*" I John 4:16-17. The Lord of heaven and earth, the one who created everything in this world, has the ability and the right to judge how He sees fit. What we need to understand is that we were created in God's image, so we can judge as well. But because of our sin nature we also possess the ability to make mistakes. Because of this condition, we need a source of information (the Bible) to help us judge properly without exceeding the balance of what God expects from us. This is where the world gets off track, going to all-or-nothing extremes when it comes to judging. People either claim to never judge or they become critical of everything and everyone.

The many scriptures directing us not to judge are referring to slandering someone. This type of judgment has only one purpose, to cause damage. If slandering and codependency get together in the same body, they will produce a very judgmental person. Criticizing, complaining, never being satisfied and being offended are some of the more common expressions of judging people. All of this comes from the condition of the heart and was the context of Jesus' words on how to address the problem. He used an analogy to describe what is in the fog, and the necessity to remove the obstacle so that we can "properly" judge. *"Why do you look at the speck of sawdust in your brother's eye and pay no attention to the plank in your own eye? How can you say to your brother, 'Let me take the speck out of your eye,' when all the time there is a plank in your own eye? You hypocrite, first take the plank out of your own eye, and then you will see clearly to remove the speck from your brother's eye."* Matthew 7:3-5.

The directive here is for a person who fails to recognize his or her own problems. They are externally focused on the problems of others, but not their own. Jesus says to remove our own problems first, and then we will see clearly to help other people with theirs. For example, codependents like to give unwanted advice, and generally help other people solve their problems. This scripture may explain why codependents seem to have an uncanny knack of crossing boundaries, because they cannot see clearly. Other people are already upset with them by the time they realize what they have done. Jesus is saying to clear up the internal problems first, the ones that are blinding the codependent from properly helping others. He also said the goal was to "remove the speck" from someone else's life, which requires judging that there is something to be removed.

Everyone should have at least one other person who has an open door to confront a problem in his or her life. It is better to have more than one, but just two or three is enough. This means that trust has been placed in another person to judge our lives, and speak if there is a concern. A familiar scripture reads, "*As iron sharpens iron, so one person sharpens another.*" Proverbs 27:17. Save the warm and fuzzies for a group hug, because when iron sharpens iron sparks fly. The picture here is one of friction sharpening a sword, enough to produce change in the character of the weapon. The final condition will be one of value and quality; a dull sword is ineffective. In order to make the decision to sharpen a sword, a judgment has to be made that it needs work. Occasionally, we need someone to point out the speck, a problem that needs to be removed. Those who claim to never judge will either be unable to have this type of trust in another person, or they will have to contradict themselves to obtain it. The truth is we need to judge, and to be judged.

Finding the balance of discernment in judging as it applies to overcoming codependency can be done through a simple review of some Bible commentaries, and a little study of the Strong's concordance. It supports the idea of having a balance between the extremes. There are two Greek words that are used commonly in the New Testament for judging.

- One refers to an attitude: "literally, judging 'back-and-forth' which can either (positively) refer to close-reasoning or negatively 'over-judging'."
- The other refers to a position of judging: "come to a choice (decision, judgment) by making a judgment – either positive (a verdict in favor of) or negative (which rejects or condemns)."

- A Bible commentator (J. Thayer) wrote: "intelligent comparison and contrast based on God's word, i.e. to approve (prefer) what is correct and reject what is inferior (wrong)." (Strong's concordance - #2919)
- Another commentator (Elliot) wrote about Matthew 7:1. "*Must we not, even as a matter of duty, be judging others every day of our lives? The juryman giving his verdict, the master who discharges a dishonest servant, the bishop who puts in force the discipline of the Church—are these acting against our Lord's commands? And if not, where are we to draw the line?*"
- In regard to judging people based on appearance Jesus said "*Stop judging by mere appearances, but instead judge correctly.*" John 7:24.
- Barnes commentary on John 7:24. "*This expression is to be understood as meaning that he judged no one after their manner; he did not come to censure and condemn men after the appearance, or in a harsh, biased, and unkind manner.*"

From these commentators and Greek references we can draw some conclusions for the subject of judging in regard to codependency. We are neither called to avoid judging or to over-judge. Attention is focused on the contrast between positive and negative, and what is right vs. what is wrong. A word that is used is "reasoning," which is exactly what we would expect from a person who is a judge in a court of law. We are to use sound reasoning when judging between right and wrong, truth and lies, dependency and codependency. Our source of information to accomplish this is the Bible, which challenges us to remove the obstacles that blind us and become more like Jesus. Then we can approve what is correct and reject what is wrong.

The scripture in John 7:24 states both types of judging, to avoid slandering through judging people by their appearance, and to make a correct judgment based on the whole person. Codependency judges the world by the external conditions, which is why codependents are so judgmental towards people who are different in their appearance. Remove the plank of codependency and then a clear judgment can be made based on the internal condition of a person. Some people are not safe; we have to judge that condition with clear motives. God looks at the heart, and He wants us to do the same.

We also know that since God created us with a brain, it is safe to assume He expects us to use it to judge. Improper application of the subject of judging and codependency can be life threatening, because people will allow unsafe people into their lives, and remain in relationships that they should get out of. The heart will override the mind, reflected in the common situation of codependent people "knowing" they should get out of a harmful relationship, but "feeling" like they cannot. These can be the hardest people to help. They need to judge, but don't. They are addicted to the relationship, they are codependent.

"The secret of sin is that it fuels codependency and blocks off access to the third option." It hides inside of our secrets, increases our sensitivity to being offended, and distorts our God-given ability to judge. Meanwhile the father of lies uses it not only against Christians, but also against any human being. Finding the balance between the extremes is possible when the planks are removed from our spiritual eyes.

Are you ready for surgery?

6

The Most Codependent Man
and Woman in the Bible

There are two people in the Bible, one woman and one man, whose lives provide insights into the problem of codependency as well as the solution. While they are not the only examples of codependency in Scripture, they are the best to study regarding this issue. But before getting to those, there are a couple other examples worth studying.

The Seven Sons of Sceva.

"Some Jews who went around driving out evil spirits tried to invoke the name of the Lord Jesus over those who were demon-possessed. They would say, 'In the name of the Jesus whom Paul preaches, I command you to come out.' Seven sons of Sceva, a Jewish chief priest, were doing this. One day the evil spirit answered them, 'Jesus I know, and Paul I know about, but who are you?' Then the man who had the evil spirit jumped on them and overpowered them all." Acts 19:13-16.

The Seven Sons of Sceva were depending on a spirit they did not have, calling him Jesus. The story indicates that they were actually having some level of success, until one day when they met a certain evil spirit. It seems they were depending upon their heritage and their father's position in the synagogue, and perhaps on the number of brothers in their family. In any case, it was not enough and was revealed as dependency on the wrong source and not on God. *Codependency occurs anytime dependence exceeds the limits that God has established.* In this case, it was being expressed in the name of Jesus and exceeded the ability of those using the name. It was exposed when the problem became bigger than the codependents.

Christian codependents have often been in church for a long time, and even though they have reached the level of "flaming," they are still in denial over the problem. Maybe an older member of their family is a prominent leader; perhaps there are a large number of other family members in the church. It could be that some level of success in ministry has produced a confidence that God is empowering them. Their heritage is rich with serving, but their codependent nature will eventually meet a force it cannot overcome. Unfortunately, when these people are confronted the common response is to complain about what other people are doing, the ones who in their opinion are the real problem. One such person was heard saying how his church needed to get rid of all that "seven eleven" music. He was complaining that the new music was the same seven words eleven times. He might have to complain in heaven too, since Revelation 4:8 says *"Day and night they never stop saying: 'Holy, holy, holy is the Lord God Almighty, who was, and is, and is to come.'"* Evidently heaven didn't get the memo about repetition. The codependent nature of long term church members is often revealed in how they deal with change.

"Claiming the name of Jesus as Savior does not prevent codependency." From the story above we can see that even people who use His name can be spiritually overpowered when an evil force exceeds their abilities. We know that the forces of evil will never overpower Jesus himself, so the problem is not with Him or His name, the problem is with us. The Apostle Paul depended on the power of God and was successful. The seven sons of Sceva exceeded

the limits of what God could do through them, and they failed. Codependents in the church often take on roles they are not gifted or qualified for, but because Jesus' name is on the task it must be right. The goal is to receive external recognition and accolades as a way to compensate for internal problems, but the person is externally being viewed as a faithful servant.

The seven sons must have felt pretty good about themselves at first, perhaps even gained some recognition. That all changed when one man with an evil spirit overpowered all seven of them. They must have been embarrassed or at least humbled after that. When people experience failure, they can blame the circumstances and stay the same, or they can become humble and change. Christian servants who are truly dependent on God will not have the same results as Christian servants who are codependent. The problems can show up gradually over time, or they can be exposed quickly through a crisis.

Paul on the Road to Damascus

The book of Acts Chapters 9, 22, & 26 tell about an experience Paul had on the road to Damascus, when God deliberately blinded him. He became totally dependent upon those around him until God was ready to restore his sight, unable to even walk without help. The experience was so significant that God even changed his name from Saul to Paul. The old person Saul thought he was depending on God and doing the divine work of attacking the problems in the church. What God proved was that he was actually codependent, acting in dysfunctional and abusive ways in God's name. It was a crisis that broke his codependency and realigned his faith with truth. The Lord used the circumstances to show him how to depend on the true source of life.

Breaking through codependency often involves a crisis where our perceived independence is revealed as codependency.

God uses other people to help when we are blinded to our own problems, people who can guide us until we get our sight back. How many today are on their road to Damascus? They are on a reckless path of destruction in the name of God, those who refuse to yield or recognize the error of their ways. Blessed are those who find a crisis along the way, because they are given the gift of desperation. Changing direction by forced submission is better than continuing on and suffering more severe consequences. It is actually quite sad to meet people who are extremely codependent while serving God, especially when they do not have a clue how sick they really are. Most of the ones I meet are Christians, and they rarely accept help from other people who understand the problem. They are blinded by pride.

After Paul regains his sight, he never turns his back on serving God. Eventually he writes a letter to the church at Corinth, and records an insight into codependency. "*And now, brothers and sisters, we want you to know about the grace that God has given the Macedonian churches. In the midst of a very severe trial, their overflowing joy and their extreme poverty welled up in rich generosity. For I testify that they gave as much as they were able, and even beyond their ability. Entirely on their own, they urgently pleaded with us for the privilege of sharing in this service to the Lord's people.*" II Corinthians 8:1-4. In these words we find an example of people who wanted to help support Paul's ministry even though they were poor. The application is for those who have recognized their own codependent problems, have found a solution, and will consider it a privilege to share that solution with others. What they need is a person who has enough honesty to admit they are sick and will accept help.

Until we realize that we are in a position of deep poverty in regard to God's grace, we will not properly understand our dependence on Him, and will remain codependent to some degree. Otherwise we would beg Him for the chance to help others, even though we know of our own spiritual poverty. The Macedonian churches pleaded for the privilege to help, even though they were in the middle of extreme poverty. That is exactly what we need in the Christian churches and in our communities, an attitude of pleading with God for the privilege of helping others. It can only come from Godly dependence that starts on the inside of our hearts, when we care more about the person outside the church than the one already on the inside. This type of proper dependence is not a mindset of all-or-nothing extremes, meaning all importance or no importance, neither egotistical nor dirty rags. It represents the third option, to know how valuable we are in God's eyes, how undeserving we are of His grace, and how He gives it to us anyway. *"When it comes to codependency, we are either on our own road to Damascus, or we are guides for other people when their crisis comes."*

The Most Codependent Woman in the Bible: The Samaritan Woman

The Biblical story of the Samaritan woman is rich with truth and codependency. Sometimes this story is referred to as "The Woman at the Well," which has been depicted in some familiar pictures imagining what this event must have been like. The story involves Jesus going out of his way to make a trip to Samaria. Upon arriving he goes by himself to get water from a well while those traveling with him go to find food. There he meets a local woman who is coming to draw water, and Jesus strikes up a conversation with her. This was no chance meeting; there was a divine purpose and a plan for both of them to be there.

A few of the common portraits of this event show a young beautiful woman sitting at the feet of Jesus, looking up with eyes full of hope and wonder. Seems a little odd considering she had been married five times, decided to give up on commitment and live with her boyfriend, filled with bitterness, wanted to argue, and had a seriously bad attitude. Perhaps a portrait of a worn-out middle-aged woman with a few teeth missing would be more accurate. She is not a model of hope for women. She is a completely dysfunctional person who Jesus wanted to help. In the dialogue that takes place in John Chapter Four we learn a lot about the problem of codependency and the solution. Jesus is prepared to engage in a discussion that will be the equivalent of what we call today "an intervention." The Samaritan woman was a flaming codependent who was on a reckless path in life.

"Now he had to go through Samaria. So he came to a town in Samaria called Sychar, near the plot of ground Jacob had given to his son Joseph. Jacob's well was there, and Jesus, tired as he was from the journey, sat down by the well. It was about noon. When a Samaritan woman came to draw water, Jesus said to her, 'Will you give me a drink?' (His disciples had gone into the town to buy food.) The Samaritan woman said to him, 'You are a Jew and I am a Samaritan woman. How can you ask me for a drink?' (For Jews do not associate with Samaritans.)" John 4:4-9.

The first thing we learn is that the Samaritan woman showed up with a preexisting bad attitude; in other words, she had a chip on her shoulder. Through the course of this discussion more will be revealed about exactly what her issues are, but for now we discover that she thinks she is "unique." A common phrase used in recovery to describe people who have this problem is "terminal uniqueness." They are different from everyone else, and nobody understands the problems they are facing, or so they think. For many it is a consuming problem that blinds them to other issues in their life, and the outcome is codependency. Jesus simply asked for some water, and the first thing this woman points out is the differences between them. Her bad attitude is immediately revealed as someone trying to be unique and different from other people.

She also takes it a step further in saying, "How can you ask me?" While this could be understood as clarifying their differences, it can also be viewed as an attitude of "who are you to tell me?" It would be easy to picture her saying this with one hand on her hip, the other hand pointing a finger, and her head bobbing side to side. Codependents are quick to be defensive when establishing their uniqueness. It does not take much to trigger this response, because it is ready at all times to be used for protection against intruders. It is the Skunk from Chapter Two. The Samaritan woman did not want to associate with Jesus, a condition made obvious by her first statements that were in response to a simple and reasonable question. Another common trait of codependents is making a big response to a simple question and acting like the other person is the problem. It is important to note that Jesus responds by over-looking her offensive attitude and redirecting the conversation.

"Jesus answered her, 'If you knew the gift of God and who it is that asks you for a drink, you would have asked him and he would have given you living water.'" John 4:10. Notice that Jesus does not try to chase her around the discussion; instead He guides the topic. This approach is effective in communicating with codependents who want to avoid focusing on the subject at hand. Changing the subject to avoid truth is a common tool for codependents. Staying focused on the subject matter is a good response. Adding truth and clarity to the discussion is also effective. Jesus catches her interest by talking about "living water." Her response is classic.

"'Sir,' the woman said, 'You have nothing to draw with and the well is deep. Where can you get this living water? Are you greater than our father Jacob, who gave us the well and drank from it him-self, as did also his sons and his livestock?'" John 4:11-12.

Here we see two other issues: she likes to argue and does not listen. The statement Jesus made was actually about him as the gift of God, but she only hears two words about living water and reacts with more of her bad attitude. Whether it is passive or aggressive, controlling or avoiding, flaming or mild, codependents argue and do not listen. Some will say things to your face, others behind your back, but what they all fail to recognize is the condition existed before the discussion ever started. An old saying that fits well with this problem is to "take the cotton out of your ears and put it in your mouth," which would provide a chance to stop talking and start listening. This would have been good advice for the woman at the well.

Have you ever listened to a radio program that helps people with problems in life? If so, then you have heard the Samaritan woman call in and ask for help. The caller will go into great detail about their struggles, describing difficult circumstances and making an emotional appeal for help. Then, as soon as the host of the program begins to answer their questions, the caller will join in and try to help provide the answer. If by chance they do actually listen, they will validate the host's answer by saying they have already done or said whatever is being suggested. The caller is actually exposing their own codependency while at the same time being completely unaware of what they are doing, just like the woman at the well. A good host will remain engaged in the discussion while trying to guide the person towards a solution, the same as Jesus does throughout this story.

The problem of arguing for the codependent goes hand in hand with not listening. It is very common to provide answers for people struggling with codependency, only to have them argue about the solution. Another response is to claim the person providing the solution doesn't know what they are talking about. This happens when the discussion gets too honest. The attention is focused on the messenger to avoid the message. Since Jesus has already planted the seed of a message about living water, He again moves away from her response and provides more truth about the real subject.

"Jesus answered, 'Everyone who drinks this water will be thirsty again, but whoever drinks the water I give them will never thirst. Indeed, the water I give them will become in them a spring of water welling up to eternal life.'" John 4:13-14.

How appropriate it would have been for Jesus to jump right to the end of the discussion, and respond to her previous statement that he was in fact greater than Jacob. Instead He takes just one small and calculated step towards the goal. What is important to understand is that Jesus has a plan and a purpose for the discussion. He is keeping the end goal in mind, one that we will learn about later. For now He wants her to focus on something greater than life itself. *"Jesus used the physical to describe the spiritual, the tangible to describe the intangible."* It is a tool that works well in communicating with codependents about their issues.

This principle ties back to the idea of asking a codependent if they *"can violate God's Word and receive a blessing."* The end goal of a discussion with a codependent is to help the person see a solution when they are emotionally enmeshed in the problem. The typical example is when they are enabling someone's addictive behavior. Trying to cut right to the end result does not work too well, since it is too big of a gap to cover in one question or statement. Presenting this question helps to shift the codependent's attention from the physical to the spiritual, the tangible to the intangible. Shifting to spiritual principles and the potential blessings is a way to get through the denial. However in this Bible story, the Samaritan woman still has a long way to go.

"'The woman said to him, 'Sir, give me this water so that I won't get thirsty and have to keep coming here to draw water.'" John 4:15.

The next issues we see for the Samaritan woman are that of being "demanding and overwhelmed." Jesus now has her attention, sort of. She at least heard what he said about the living water, but turns it into a self-focused demand to lighten her burdens. At this point it would have been a healthy response to simply ask Jesus what he was talking about. But she is not a healthy person, and her multiple issues are still in the process of being revealed. Notice that she doesn't even have the decency to ask; she just demands that Jesus give her the water. The reason given is so she won't have the chore of getting water for her home. She's overloaded and finds a way to blame the water.

Codependents will overload their own lives and then believe if they just had one more thing it would solve their problems. Blaming external conditions for being overwhelmed is common. They will point to all that they do for other people when they are the ones who decided to do more than they are capable of. In solving these problems a codependent can become demanding. Their external focus is convinced that the solution is outside of them, revealed in this story by demanding living water. The Samaritan woman had no idea what she was asking for, but she wanted it anyway. She was confused to say the least. Codependents that are demanding and overwhelmed are quite often confused, and even though they have no idea what they need, they will demand something anyway. Cooperation from others is usually at the top of the list, but it can be anything from respect to money to needing a break or a vacation. The list is endless.

At this point Jesus uses another technique that is effective in dealing with codependents: He shifts the conversation to the next step of truth. They have discussed the water issue enough, and even though she already wants what Jesus is offering, there are still a few more issues to deal with.

"*He told her, 'Go, call your husband and come back.' 'I have no husband,' she replied. Jesus said to her, 'You are right when you say you have no husband. The fact is, you have had five husbands, and the man you now have is not your husband. What you have just said is quite true.'*" John 4:16-18.

The Samaritan woman has "secrets." Jesus already knew about her current and past relationships, but chooses to ask a question without revealing His insights. In doing so, He gives us another communication tool in dealing with codependency. Sometimes the best approach is to ask a question you already know the answer to. This is not for the purpose of being clever or deceitful; the wall of denials can be hard to break through. It should be used when the goal is to help the other person see something they are hiding. If this approach is actually bad or deceitful, then Jesus committed a sin, which we know is impossible. A wise and discerning person will know when and where to use this approach. Counselors use this tool all the time, because they can see things their client cannot. But they need to guide the discussion through the problems to reveal the self-deception or denial. It can be used to guide the conversation towards a solution where jumping straight to the end would only cause damage to the codependent.

Jesus has now revealed that He is not just some ordinary guy who stopped by for a drink of water. The Samaritan woman has the chance to give up the struggle and the debate, but instead only manages to reveal more of her problems.

"'Sir,' the woman said, 'I can see that you are a prophet. Our ancestors worshipped on this mountain, but you Jews claim that the place where we must worship is in Jerusalem.'" John 4:19-20

She now reveals one of the most common codependent responses to truth, by becoming a "victim." Even though Jesus just cut through her deceit by accurately telling her about her past, she can only manage a brief acknowledgement that he is right. She got caught telling a half-truth and decides to put a spin on the subject. In part this connects back to the first issue of being unique, by pointing out the differences between them. However, she takes it to another level by bringing in the whole ancestry of the nation. Not only is she unique, but her people are the victims of his people.

The victim role is a byproduct of codependency. The cause can be real or imagined; some people will create the role of victim out of partial truth, others out of pure denial. There is a difference between true victims and false ones, but even true victims have a choice of moving beyond the cause and not remaining a victim. Codependency will take away that choice because the role depends on taking something external and making it an internal problem. The Samaritan woman was quick to play the victim role, which means that she was used to doing it already. She didn't just suddenly think of it as a response, she was out of excuses and used the only one she had left. Jesus now arrives at the truth that He has

been working towards the whole time. If He had given her the following message up front, her own codependent issues would have
rejected it. She would have argued, not listened, become demanding, and hid behind her secrets. Jesus wore out all her excuses first,
and then gives her the gift of "hope."

*"'Woman,' Jesus replied, 'believe me, a time is coming when
you will worship the Father neither on this mountain nor in Jerusalem. You Samaritans worship what you do not know; we worship
what we do know, for salvation is from the Jews. Yet a time is coming
and has now come when the true worshipers will worship the Father
in the Spirit and in truth, for they are the kind of worshipers the
Father seeks. God is spirit, and his worshipers must worship in the
Spirit and in truth.' The woman said, 'I know that Messiah' (called
Christ) 'is coming. When he comes, he will explain everything to
us.' Then Jesus declared, 'I, the one speaking to you—I am he.'"*
John 4:21-26.

Could you imagine if Jesus had said at the beginning of the
story that He was the Messiah? She probably would have laughed
and left. But before this dialogue ever took place, even before Jesus
arrived in her town, the story says, *"Now he had to go through
Samaria."* He knew where He was going, who He was going to see
and what she was going to be like. In this statement He acknowl-
edges the differences between them, but focuses on the similarities
instead. It would seem at this point in the story that the goal had
been accomplished, especially when she believed what Jesus said
about Himself. But there is more. The codependency of the Samaritan woman is only part of the picture, a greater truth is revealed
as the story continues.

*"Then, leaving her water jar, the woman went back to the
town and said to the people, 'Come, see a man who told me everything I ever did. Could this be the Messiah?' They came out of the
town and made their way toward him. ...Many of the Samaritans from that town believed in him because of the woman's testimony, 'He told me everything I ever did.' So when the Samaritans*

came to him, they urged him to stay with them, and he stayed two days. And because of his words many more became believers." John 4:28-30, 39-41.

The Samaritan woman becomes an evangelist, or did she? After Jesus wears out her excuses, after she believes that He is the Messiah, she leaves the water jar and heads back to town. Suddenly this woman full of problems who has been married five times, and who probably doesn't have the best reputation in town, goes to spread the news that the greatest promise from God is actually sitting at Jacob's well just outside of their hometown. The story says "many" of them came; she must have been very convincing. As a result many became believers in Jesus.

The real ending of this story is that a woman who was full of sin and secrets became compassionate about people. But she did not suddenly become an evangelist, she always was one. Codependency will change a person from the inside out. It will take God-given spiritual gifts and render them useless. Satan cannot take away the spiritual gifts that God grants to each person, He can only cause damage and keep him or her from being used. The Samaritan woman had the gifts of compassion and mercy, demonstrated by what happened after Jesus removed all the barriers. The wall of denial was destroyed, the truth broke through and set her free, and she cared about people. This story is for "many" who are codependents, because they have spiritual gifts of compassion and mercy that are being destroyed by codependency. They can be people who already believe in God and are trying to serve Him, but desperately need emotional and spiritual healing. The woman at the well knew about the Messiah, yet she lived without hope and was filled with bitterness. There are many in churches today just like her. It is a story for both men and women.

The final issue that is revealed through the Samaritan woman is that "healing" came to a sick person. To arrive at healing a codependent must go through a process of revealing truth and confronting obstacles. It usually involves another person who can "*speak the truth in love*" Ephesians 4:15. Most codependents want a quick fix just like a drug addict, because they do not understand the depth of their illness. This problem affects a person spiritually, emotionally, mentally, and physically. Underestimating the problem is part of the problem. But what if a codependent could understand that their God given gifts were being used against them? And that the one who was doing this was actually their enemy? Just knowing this will not resolve all the issues, but it should provide the motivation to face whatever is in the fog.

It seems that a large number of codependents have the same basic characteristic as the Samaritan woman, spiritual gifts of compassion and mercy. The proof is in how many are working in professions of caring — health care for humans and animals, as well as organizations that rescue both people and animals; people in church, ministry, and missionaries that give their lives to see others saved for eternity; counselors, therapists, and even lawyers who care about their clients. Mothers see their roles as caretakers for the family, and fathers want to be the providers. Certainly this does not apply to all codependents; some are just controllers who don't work in roles that help others at all. But "many" who are codependent spend a great deal of their lives involved in helping and caring. It is their God-given desire and gift, which explains why so many codependents are stressed and overwhelmed. The gifts of compassion and mercy are buried beneath layers of dysfunction, unfulfilled and straining to get out. It is like holding a beach ball under water; after a while you get tired and can't do it anymore. Instead of facing the problem, a person quits. The Samaritan woman desperately wanted a loving dependent relationship, and quit five times.

The Lord put this woman to the test. He knew that she was being oppressed by a problem that needed an answer, and went out of His way to provide it. Maybe she prayed for a solution, maybe not, we aren't told one way or another. What we know is that she had to face her problems to find healing. No more blaming, secrets, or being a victim, just surrender and acceptance. Her problems had two basic characteristics; they were internal and had developed over time. The Samaritan woman was a flaming codependent who had an intervention.

The Most Codependent Man in the Bible: Moses

One of the greatest men who ever walked the earth was Moses. He was used by God to lead the Israelites out of Egypt, a task that involved more than a million people. He also possessed some of the same characteristics that have been listed throughout this book. Even though he made great decisions and had faith beyond measure, he was also the most codependent man in the Bible. He was more of a "mild" codependent, similar to most men with codependency. While there are examples of men who are flaming codependents, they tend to be the lesser percentage. As for Moses, he was overwhelmed, tried to do more than he could, and as a result received an intervention. At other times he tried to quit and even asked God to take his life, but remained in his leadership role instead. Eventually Moses paid a heavy price for the consequences of his codependency. Men who serve in leadership roles and remain codependent will pay a price as well.

In Exodus chapter 18 there is a story about Moses, which takes place with the Israelite community in the desert. His wife has gone to see her father Jethro, and took two of their sons with her. Eventually Jethro comes with his daughter and grandchildren to see Moses in the desert, and provides an intervention when he sees what his son-in-law is doing. The story contains insights for men in particular who are codependent.

"After Moses had sent away his wife Zipporah, his father-in-law Jethro received her and her two sons. .... Jethro, Moses' father-in-law, together with Moses' sons and wife, came to him in the wilderness, where he was camped near the mountain of God. Jethro

had sent word to him, 'I, your father-in-law Jethro, am coming to you with your wife and her two sons.'" Exodus 18:2-6.

The first thing we see is that Moses doesn't know when to take time off from his work. He sent his family away but remains behind, and the only way his father-in-law gets to see him is to go into the wilderness where Moses is. Men who are codependent often tie their identity to their work, so much so that the family is neglected or abandoned. Many books have been written about this characteristic, trying to get men to change their ways and put their family first. Some of these writings have even focused on the fact that men bring their role at work home and try to be the same with their family as they are with their co-workers. But few of these resources have properly labeled the problem as being male codependency. A close look at the life of Moses will bring clarity, insights, and solutions.

The story tells us that Moses sent his family away but stayed behind. If that was all we knew then very few conclusions could be pulled from this account. But it is what his father-in-law finds him doing after he arrives that completes the picture. *"The next day Moses took his seat to serve as judge for the people, and they stood around him from morning till evening. When his father-in-law saw all that Moses was doing for the people, he said, 'What is this you are doing for the people? Why do you alone sit as judge, while all these people stand around you from morning till evening?'* "Exodus 18:13-14.

Jethro had to travel into the desert just to see Moses, and finds him consumed in his work from morning until evening. Here we can see why Moses did not take time away to go with his family, because he gave all his time to his vocation. Men today will do the same thing, claiming somehow they have to provide for their family and use a host of reasons why the situation cannot change. Moses tries the same thing with Jethro, but it did not work.

"Moses answered him, 'Because the people come to me to seek God's will. Whenever they have a dispute, it is brought to me,

and I decide between the parties and inform them of God's decrees and instructions.' Moses' father-in-law replied, 'What you are doing is not good. You and these people who come to you will only wear yourselves out. The work is too heavy for you; you cannot handle it alone.'" Exodus 18:15-18.

Normally it takes someone who is not wrapped up in the problem to point out the solution. Codependents often feel trapped in their roles and fail to see any answers. Men do this with their work, or other volunteer roles such as coaching sports or leading civic groups. The common characteristic is to believe that if they don't fill the role then no one will. So they just keep doing the same thing over and over until it is too much. Jethro comes along and tells Moses what he is doing is wrong and needs to change. From the way this story transpires it is clear Moses was not going to make any changes without some type of intervention. His excuse is logical but still wrong. Reading a little into the dialogue shows Moses thought he was the only one who could properly judge, a condition of "uniqueness," the same as the Samaritan Woman.

Corporate environments are a breeding ground for this type of codependency. What we need to keep in mind is that God did not establish corporations, He established the family. Healthy dependence starts in our relationship with Him, then our family, ministry, and finally at work. When people get this order backwards there is role reversal, what is good will become bad and what is bad will become good. Godly dependency is replaced with employer dependence, an external source of validation that is constantly changing. When men get their sense of self-worth at work the result will be codependency. There is plenty of recognition for codependents who sacrifice their own health and families to climb the corporate ladder, but many do not like what they find at the top.

The plant that I worked at for 20 years started as a family-owned business and over time was purchased by a large corporation. The company went from about 200 employees to 1,400.

During the several years that this growth took place, many oppor-tunities opened up and made it possible for people to be promoted into management. It was during that time that I transitioned from an hourly employee to a salaried manager. Even with my familiarity with the plant and job requirements, there was always something new to learn with advancement. Part of mine was to face expecta-tions that started coming from those who were above me on the corporate ladder.

I worked hard to get my management responsibilities done within a 40-hour workweek, and I did. When it was time to go home, I went home. Not too long after becoming a manager I was confronted by more senior management about not working 50 to 60 hours a week as most of the other managers did. It seems part of the problem was that people who had been in management much longer than I had were working more hours than I was, and the solution was for me to work more hours as well. There were times I worked long hours or stayed late, which was not a problem. But to do it on a regular basis for no other purpose than satisfy another person, no thanks. I was not going to take that time away from my family and give it to work just to please somebody. When push came to shove I simply asked one question, "What part of my job am I not doing?" Since there was no answer to that ques-tion there was no change in my hours. I was getting everything done that needed to be done in the time I was there. That period of time took place around the middle of the 20-year span. After that I was promoted and given increased responsibilities several times, partly because of having the reputation of working hard and getting results.

I encountered people during the same time frame who believed that taking such a stand with the employer was a career killer, and that such a person would never get ahead. I chose to put God first, my family second, ministry third, and job fourth. *"Proper dependence produces proper results, something codepen-dency can never provide."* During that time I also observed people who were "yes men," the kind that said yes to everything as a way to demonstrate their commitment to the company. The problem is these people operate without boundaries, because they fail to say "no" when they should. This type of person thinks they will get promoted for their eagerness to always do more and never refuse a request. The reality is they rarely get promoted, because they take on too much responsibility and are known as the people that complete their work late, or not at all.

Moses needed a vacation and stayed at work instead. He was working more hours than he should and still did not get his work done. Instead of searching for an answer he just kept on doing what he was doing, the same thing day after day. He was headed for a crash, sometimes referred to as "burnout." Getting a codependent to change their ways is difficult; sometimes they just have to "crash and burn" to stop. Maybe they have a nervous breakdown or some other health problem. A friend of mine who has been working through his own male codependency went to a doctor because he was fatigued and it was affecting his work, much of which was outdoors. The doctor told him, "You're not supposed to look like that," referring to his sun-dried reptile skin. He was not taking care of himself, but was trying to take care of everyone else. Sound familiar? Codependents like Moses will get their priorities mixed up and try to do more than they can for others while neglecting themselves. Jethro was right on time and gave some valuable advice.

"Listen now to me and I will give you some advice, and may God be with you. You must be the people's representative before God and bring their disputes to him. Teach them his decrees and instructions, and show them the way they are to live and how they are to behave. But select capable men from all the people—men who fear God, trustworthy men who hate dishonest gain—and appoint them as officials over thousands, hundreds, fifties and tens. Have them serve as judges for the people at all times, but have them bring every difficult case to you; the simple cases they can decide

themselves. That will make your load lighter, because they will share it with you. If you do this and God so commands, you will be able to stand the strain, and all these people will go home satisfied." Exodus 18:19-23.

There is no doubt that Moses was a great man of God, but even he needed advice when codependency got in the way. Jethro starts out by validating Moses' role for the Israelites, as their teacher and representative before God. He then tells Moses to "teach" the people and "show them the way" to follow God, instead of depending on him all the time. Then Jethro provides a solution that is not only wise, but is actually the principle upon which the court systems of America were established centuries later. A system of judges is suggested, ones with higher and lower responsibilities, with the more difficult situations eventually coming to Moses. He was the model of the U.S. Supreme Court. This structure is also given as one that will relieve the strain on Moses, but he has a decision to make. Will he listen or argue?

"Moses listened to his father-in-law and did everything he said. He chose capable men from all Israel and made them leaders of the people, officials over thousands, hundreds, fifties and tens. They served as judges for the people at all times. The difficult cases they brought to Moses, but the simple ones they decided themselves. Then Moses sent his father-in-law on his way, and Jethro returned to his own country." Exodus 18:24-27.

The comparison here is when someone with insight gives the codependent a solution. In this case Moses listened and found a solution to his problems. Simple but profound, the answers to codependency are rarely complicated; they just require a person who is willing to listen and follow directions from someone else who understands the problem. Moses was a mild codependent, demonstrated by the fact that even though he had the characteristics of the problem, he still had the ability to listen, follow directions, and change. Male codependents that are confronted but fail to listen or change will pay a price for their resistance.

There was another time that Moses displayed codependent traits. In Numbers Chapter 15 he actually wanted God to kill him over frustration with the Israelites. The story follows the idea of "Look at all that I'm doing, and this is the thanks I get." It was all about external circumstances that were beyond Moses' control and were overwhelming to him. He results to sarcasm with God and having an emotional melt down.

"Moses heard the people of every family wailing at the entrance to their tents. The LORD *became exceedingly angry, and Moses was troubled. He asked the* LORD, *'Why have you brought this trouble on your servant? What have I done to displease you that you put the burden of all these people on me? Did I conceive all these people? Did I give them birth? Why do you tell me to carry them in my arms, as a nurse carries an infant, to the land you promised on oath to their ancestors? Where can I get meat for all these people? They keep wailing to me, 'Give us meat to eat!' I cannot carry all these people by myself; the burden is too heavy for me. If this is how you are going to treat me, please go ahead and kill me—if I have found favor in your eyes—and do not let me face my own ruin.'"* Numbers 15:10-15.

This is something that must have built up over time. Moses blames the people's request for meat as the reason for his comments and attitude, but only points out the codependent nature of his remarks. Can you imagine that Moses would actually want to die over the people wanting meat? This is the guy who saw the 10 plagues in Egypt, who witnessed firsthand the parting of the Red Sea, and saw bread from heaven appear every morning. Why such a lack of faith now? Why the sarcasm about giving birth? What we learn from this account is that the effects of codependency will come and go, increase and decrease, or come in cycles of highs and lows. Just because a person makes progress with codependency in one area does not mean they won't have challenges in another. It is also possible to make progress and then become complacent with the same problem. These issues have a way of coming up out of nowhere later. The good news is that tools for codependency do not wear out; sometimes they just need to be picked up again and used. God provides a solution to Moses' problem that is similar to the story in Exodus 18.

"The Lord said to Moses: 'Bring me seventy of Israel's elders who are known to you as leaders and officials among the people. Have them come to the tent of meeting, that they may stand there with you. I will come down and speak with you there, and I will take some of the power of the Spirit that is on you and put it on them. They will share the burden of the people with you so that you will not have to carry it alone.'" Numbers 15:16-17.

The Lord's answer to the problem was for Moses to share the load of the work. Once again he is trying to do everything himself. The order of events in the life of Moses is not the point, but the reoccurrence of his codependent character is. He remained a great man of God while continuing to fall back on codependent weaknesses. What kept him from progressing into a flaming codependent was his ability to hear truth and respond. Examples from the Bible do not always need to be from stories of failure, where a person just keeps going until a disaster happens. Moses is an example of someone who had personal struggles with issues of codependency, but remained faithful to God. Mild codependents can do the same, flaming ones rarely do.

The next example from the life of Moses takes place in Numbers chapter 20. It would be difficult to see the codependency in this story without first reviewing Exodus Chapter 18 and Numbers Chapter 15. But with an understanding of Moses' struggles with the Israelites, his comments can be understood as more than just anger. This in and of itself is an insight into codependency, because people who struggle with this issue very often vent anger at those around them. Whether it is a Skunk, a Projector, the Killer Poodle, or some other characteristic, anger is a common expression for codependents. What may be of more importance here though is the price Moses pays for his anger. It seems like an innocent response out of frustration, but God didn't think so.

"Now there was no water for the community, and the people gathered in opposition to Moses and Aaron. They quarreled with Moses and said, 'If only we had died when our brothers fell dead before the LORD! Why did you bring the LORD's community into this wilderness, that we and our livestock should die here? Why did you bring us up out of Egypt to this terrible place? It has no grain or figs, grapevines or pomegranates. And there is no water to drink!' Moses and Aaron went from the assembly to the entrance to the tent of meeting and fell facedown, and the glory of the LORD appeared to them. The LORD said to Moses, 'Take the staff, and you and your brother Aaron gather the assembly together. Speak to that rock before their eyes and it will pour out its water. You will bring water out of the rock for the community so they and their livestock can drink.'" Numbers 20:2-8.

From the time the nation of Israel left Egypt they have been complaining. At times the Bible records that Moses responded with dignity and wisdom, at other times with sarcasm. This time he and Aaron simply go before the Lord and receive an answer. But Moses is holding onto bitterness and resentment towards the people, which is revealed in his actions that follow. The common powerful tool for codependent recovery is to "Let go and let God." It only works if both parts are used. Trying to let go of the problem without letting God have control will not work, neither will trying to let God have control of the problem without letting go ourselves. Moses tries the halfway approach by letting God have control, but he didn't let go of his own bitterness.

"So Moses took the staff from the LORD's presence, just as he commanded him. He and Aaron gathered the assembly together in front of the rock and Moses said to them, 'Listen, you rebels, must we bring you water out of this rock?' Then Moses raised his arm and struck the rock twice with his staff. Water gushed out, and the community and their livestock drank. But the LORD said to Moses

and Aaron, 'Because you did not trust in me enough to honor me as holy in the sight of the Israelites, you will not bring this community into the land I give them.'" Numbers 20:9-12.

There are always consequences to outburst of anger, especially public ones. Codependents try to hide their problems behind a wall of isolation, or by keeping them buried inside like "dead men's bones." Eventually the anger will come out, and it will not be pretty. At first it appears that Moses was not frustrated or struggling with anger, but when he finally speaks to the people he says, "Listen, you rebels." Turns out he was only holding his frustration down and depending on himself to control it. He let God, but he did not let go. God told him to speak to the rock and he decides to hit it instead. The outcome is a public display of Moses throwing a fit, when he takes the staff and hits the rock not once but twice. God honored His side of the solution and provides water, but since Moses failed to follow instructions he will not enter the Promised Land. There was a consequence for his anger.

Public displays of codependency are seldom pretty. The events and type of expression can and will vary, but the common trait is one of venting internal issues that have not been resolved. If the codependent blames the circumstances and other people for their actions, the cycle will continue to repeat and get worse over time. *"Fools give full vent to their rage,"* says Proverbs 29:11, a picture of a volcano erupting. A volcano that explodes causes damage to the surrounding area. When God loses His proper place of dependence in our lives, we lose as well. Anger is just one issue; lust creeps in and before long a man's first love is his car, sports team, recreation, or his job. There is nothing wrong with any of these items, unless they have been elevated to a higher priority than God and family. One positive lesson to learn from this story about Moses is that he did not blame anyone; he simply accepted the consequences of his actions. This is an example for all codependents to follow, but applies especially for men.

The Samaritan Woman and Moses are not the only examples of codependency in the Bible, but they are the best ones because of the lessons we learn. Their stories are recorded for those who have similar character flaws, and yet hold the same desire to seek God and serve Him. Codependency is not just a word for television talk shows. It has been around for centuries.

Are you ready for a solid solution?

7

The Psalm 51 Solution

Every problem we face as humans has a solution within the Bible. The solutions for codependency are provided but may require some study, just like the problem of codependency is identified throughout the Bible but not always easy to find. Even though many of those solutions have been provided already in this book, there is one chapter from the Old Testament that has yet to be covered, one that stands out above the rest, Psalm 51.

This portion of scripture was written by King David, one of the most honored and respected leaders of Israel. Yet the occasion for which he is writing has nothing to do with honor or respect. Psalm 51 is about the results of a story in the book of II Samuel Chapters 11 & 12, where David committed adultery with Bathsheba. He then tried to hide his sin through manipulating people under his authority, eventually resulting in the killing of her husband Uriah. Before that, David engaged in a deliberate plot to disguise his deeds, by bringing Uriah home from the battlefield so he could sleep with his wife and cover up the pregnancy. When Uriah refused to go into his house because he was more concerned with his men in battle, David resorts to getting him drunk to make Uriah forget his men and sleep with his wife.

When that doesn't work, David plots Uriah's death. It is worth noting that the King of Israel involved quite a few people in his sin of adultery and murder, from the servants in his house to the soldiers in his army.

David had many secrets and sins. His dependence on God had been replaced with a self-centered dependence on himself and other people. He involved his servants in the scheme from the beginning by having them bring Bathsheba to him, then having them spy on Uriah when he came home. Ultimately, he directed the warriors who fought with honor to lower themselves to his level by participating in Uriah's death. His deception was focused on reversing the roles, attempting to make what was bad look good. David's own lust had moved him from a place of being in balance with the will of God to a condition of disobedience that was extreme. He had obviously exceeded the limits which God established, ones with which he was quite familiar. David chose to abandon the faith of his youth for a cheap alternative.

Perhaps David was addicted to lust or maybe not; quite frankly, we don't know. But what we do know from this story is the King of Israel was definitely codependent. Consider some of the statements from previous chapters:

"Codependency occurs anytime dependence exceeds the limits that God has established."

"That is where codependency started, when dependency was set aside for something that looked desirable, believing there was something to gain."

"Codependents are externally-focused people in a constantly changing world."

"It is important to remember that many of the personal examples of codependency have nothing to do with addiction."

"It is role reversal, taking what is bad and making it look good, creating alternate rules for living outside of God's limits."

"Abandonment has to take place before codependency can exist."

If that was all we knew about this story, then very few conclusions could be drawn from it regarding the subject of codependency. But there is more, a lot more. The Prophet Nathan comes into the picture to confront the situation, *after the child is born.* This means that David spent several months with no consequences for his actions, while everyone around him obviously knew what happened. The story records that Bathsheba "mourned" for her husband's death, and *"After the time of mourning was over, David had her brought to his house, and she became his wife..."* II Samuel 11:26. The time of mourning for Israel was 30 days, an established principle from the Old Testament. So, King David commits adultery, murder, and then waits a whole 30 days to claim his new bride. At some level he must have felt satisfied, but he was living in the fog of his own conscience. There is just no way that a "man after God's own heart" could live with himself after what he had done apart from extreme denial. The king had bought the lie.

David just continued living in the fog until he received an intervention. He probably used avoidance to address the subject of shame until the Prophet Nathan showed up; otherwise, how could he walk past his servants on a daily basis and not repent? His denial had to increase gradually over time; after all, he also saw Bathsheba every day as the child grew in her womb. The Prophet was granted specific insight into the exact details of David's sin, but the intervention does not take place until several months later after the child is born. This was a reflection of God knowing what happened but choosing His own timing to address the problem. Nathan did not deal with David in a manner that was tender and careful as not to hurt his feelings; David was dealt with like a man who had hurt other people and needed an aggressive confrontation. But just to show David how much he was living in the fog, Nathan tells him a story about a little lamb that was the precious pet of a poor owner until some rich scoundrel killed it. The fog of David's denial was so thick that he burns with anger about the little lamb story, never getting a clue until Nathan says, "You are the man."

Eventually David hears that he will live but the child Bathsheba bore will die. "*Do not be deceived: God cannot be mocked. A man reaps what he sows.*" Galatians 6:7.

Prior to the sin David needed validation, probably because he was supposed to be in the battlefield with his men instead of being a "peeping Tom" to his neighbor's wife. He mixed up his acquaintance card with his intimacy card and used it in a place where it should not have been used, and then uses his friendship card to manipulate other people. He moves from healthy to dysfunctional, a process that started before the sin took place. People do not suddenly fall into codependency, it grows over time.

It took a crisis to get David out of his denial. He had brought shame not only on himself but also his household, nation, and Lord. Even though David listened to Nathan and accepted the consequences, the child born to Bathsheba died seven days later just as the Prophet said. Can you imagine what this woman went through in the course of one year? A pregnancy conceived in adultery, the death of her husband, and now the death of her child, all because of the sin of a man that she is now married to.

Consider some other comments from previous chapters:
"*God reveals sin before He judges it.*"
"*Does the codependent cause any less damage in the lives of those who love them? Is their true identity buried underneath layers of pretense, image, and trying to hide from the truth?*"
"*Can you violate a scriptural principle from the Bible and get a blessing from God?*"
The story of King David's sin is saturated with codependency. Yet in the aftermath of this tragic story, and out of the consequences, pain, and suffering caused by David, he writes Psalm 51.

Vs1. "*Have mercy on me, O God, according to your unfailing love; according to your great compassion blot out my transgressions.*
Vs2. *Wash away all my iniquity and cleanse me from my sin.*

Vs3.   *For I know my transgressions, and my sin is always before me.*

Vs4.   *Against you, you only, have I sinned and done what is evil in your sight; so you are right in your verdict and justified when you judge.*

Vs5.   *Surely I was sinful at birth, sinful from the time my mother conceived me.*

Vs6.   *Yet you desired faithfulness even in the womb; you taught me wisdom in that secret place.*

Vs7.   *Cleanse me with hyssop, and I will be clean; wash me, and I will be whiter than snow.*

Vs8.   *Let me hear joy and gladness; let the bones you have crushed rejoice.*

Vs9.   *Hide your face from my sins and blot out all my iniquity.*

Vs10.   *Create in me a pure heart, O God, and renew a steadfast spirit within me.*

Vs11.   *Do not cast me from your presence or take your Holy Spirit from me.*

Vs12.   *Restore to me the joy of your salvation and grant me a willing spirit, to sustain me.*

Vs13.   *Then I will teach transgressors your ways, so that sinners will turn back to you.*

Vs14.   *Deliver me from the guilt of bloodshed, O God, you who are God my Savior, and my tongue will sing of your righteousness.*

Vs15.   *Open my lips, Lord, and my mouth will declare your praise.*

Vs16.   *You do not delight in sacrifice, or I would bring it; you do not take pleasure in burnt offerings.*

Vs17.   *My sacrifice, O God, is a broken spirit; a broken and contrite heart you, God, will not despise."*

The full potential of this chapter in the Bible goes far beyond the subject of codependency and holds eternal truths about God and our human condition. Most Bible commentaries agree that verses 18 & 19 were added later, meaning after King David wrote the content of the first 17 verses. For the purpose of our study we will focus on verses 1 through 17 and how they apply to the subject of codependency.

The first thing David seeks is God's mercy. It would seem from the first three verses that he is just asking God to take everything away, looking for the easy way out. But verse three confirms that he is acknowledging his sins, which he "knows" and they are "always" before him. This means that David is now honest about the pain and suffering he has caused. He is accepting his condition and knows that it has to change. The washing referred to in verse two is literally the idea of repeated washings to remove stains, pointing to a thorough and intense process. It is a statement of surrender to God.

He then addresses the subject of judgment in verse four, by agreeing that his sin is actually against the Lord. Codependents that use their relationship with God to overlook their own sin need to apply this verse. They may have lived in the fog of their own conscience for a long time, but they will not experience healing until they honestly accept their condition and acknowledge that changes need to be made. Evil is contrary to God's nature, but is codependency really evil in God's sight? The answer is yes, but for the mild codependent, evil might just be a sense of false guilt. On the other hand the flaming codependent may have done evil that has hurt other people. The important point here is to not justify any expressions of codependency based on the degree of how bad it was, just that all of it is contrary to God's will.

David is also stating that the true measure of his sin is God's laws. Even if he lived in a culture that was similar to today, where role reversal is trying to justify sin by making what is bad look good, he would still be guilty in God's eyes. The scale of balance that God desires for humans has consequences for violations, whether society agrees or not. The change of heart that Psalm 51 eventually writes about cannot take place without acceptance of the true condition of codependency. *"Removal of denial has to take place prior to cleansing.*" In verse two David simply asks for a clean heart, but to receive it he must agree that the sins are against God Himself. The solution is a journey inward, not outward.

In verse five it would appear that David jumped into the victim role, blaming his condition on being a sinful man from birth. Keeping in mind that verse four is about acceptance, this next verse continues the same theme but gives reference to the fact that it starts at conception. There is no avoidance based on age or pointing to all the good things he has done. It puts to rest the codependent statement "Look at all that I do for you and this is the thanks I get," because healing is not based on performance or gratitude from others. King David had plenty of worthy accomplishments in his past, ones that helped his country and other people, but he does not try to use them to justify his wrongs.

Bringing verse six into the picture helps to complete the thought. For all of David's life God had required faithfulness and wisdom, even in the most secret place. He is talking about his heart, and confirming that it must always be faithful to God. Verse six is about truth on the inside of a person to the deepest part of the soul, where the cleansing needs to occur. Codependents that are not ready to fully accept their condition are not ready to be cleansed. David is ready.

So far this psalm has been about confession, which is agreeing with God according to His terms. In verse seven the focus shifts to prayer, the actual request that David is seeking from God. The cleansing will start on the inside, the part of a person that is hidden from other people, the heart and soul. It is also another acknowledgement of a process. There are two parts to this request; one is to use hyssop, which was a symbol of thoroughness, the other is to "wash me." The second request is related to the way clothes were cleaned when David was alive, which was literally with pounding. Put these two together and the request is one without reservation: he is asking God to completely clean him from the inside out, no matter what it takes. To bring this up to modern terms, mild codependents who could be easily injured need to be put through the gentle cycle on the washer, while flaming codependents need be put through a heavy duty wash, with a couple of rinse and spin cycles to get the job done. Either way it is a process. People who read this verse as an instant experience are still practicing denial, and will have trouble with the very next verse.

As David moves to his next request in verse eight, he makes a statement that seems strange. He wants to hear joy while rejoicing over crushed bones. Here David uses the physical to describe the spiritual, the tangible to describe the intangible. None of his bones were actually crushed by this experience, but his heart is full of the kind of pain that would come from an extreme physical injury. Codependents that deny hurting anyone else will not be able to experience what David is seeking. He does not ask God to remove the pain or to make it all better; he just wants to rejoice in his pain. It is only through an honest confession that a person could ask God for joy with pain. Genuine repentance will produce this, because what David is really seeking is to hear God's forgiveness. He is crying for his Father, as a child who is injured cries to be comforted by their earthly parent. The pain in his heart is more than he can bear. Codependents who can honestly reach this point have the greatest chance of healing.

Then, he seems to return to confession, but this is not the case. Verse nine is about the confidence that God's forgiveness is real. He is asking that as God comes close He will not hide His face because of David's sin. The word "all" is used to indicate that forgiveness is needed even beyond the current events. Full acceptance is required for full forgiveness; otherwise God is being asked to forgive something that a person is not accepting as wrong. Codependents like to share the blame with others, which is an obstacle to the type of healing that David is seeking. It literally happens when people are willing to own their part of a problem only as long as the other person is willing to own theirs. This is the point where many codependents just quit and go back to their old ways, a sad commentary given the nature of David's next request.

In verse 10 a prayer is given that only God could answer: *"Create in me a pure heart, O God."* From this point on, Psalm 51 is about the process of being restored. Without the conditions of confession and the requests in verses one through nine, restoration is not possible. One of the clichés in recovery is a quote from some of the original literature, that "God is doing for us what we could not do for ourselves." If someone was offered the chance to have a pure heart, only a fool would refuse. Most if not all codependents would love to have God remove their character defects, and to take away their dysfunctional issues. But how many are honestly ready? Those who want to jump to verse 10 are deceived. We can wish for a clean heart, but this verse is about the Creator performing the work of creating. The result is a condition verse 10 calls "steadfast," which means firm and steady. For the application of David's sin it means to not return the temptations that led to his problems in the first place. For codependent recovery it means not going back to old dysfunctional habits. It is the result of genuine change when God's principles are thoroughly applied.

The next verse is basically David praying to not be abandoned. The wording of verse 11 in the hands of a dysfunctional person will sound abusive, like God is going to withdraw His love and throw you out the door. Joshua 1:5 states *"I will never leave you nor forsake you,"* and since God does not contradict Himself we can rely on "never." Put in the context of the whole chapter, the verse is David's prayer to be cleansed and not left in his sinful state. The application for codependents is to know God's love is not conditional, He will not abandon you and He has no desire for you to remain in a dysfunctional state. All of those conditions are based on people placing their human experiences on

God's character. Codependents are particularly good at distorting God's character, defining who He is by the people they have experienced in life. A form of role reversal, where what is good becomes defined by what is bad.

People are born sinful, but codependency is learned. Healing comes when we want to return to a condition that existed before codependency. Verse 12 is a prayer for restoration, a returning to a time of joy and willingness, something that David remembers as a condition that "sustained" him. Perhaps this is why the references earlier in this chapter tie back all the way to the womb. People who grew up in dysfunctional homes may find it hard to remember a time when there was joy that sustained them in life. The application here is that everyone has the opportunity for restoration, no matter how far back you have to go. For others it may be from a period of youth that seems pleasant and filled with good memories. No matter what the conditions, hope of restoration is available for all people.

And then, there is verse 13. This is a stumbling block for codependents, because the tendency is to hear a solution and become an expert on how everyone else needs that information. Visions of grandeur will fill the minds of codependents as they picture themselves teaching all those "sinners" how to live right, not to mention how grateful other people will be for all the free advice. There is just one obvious problem that Psalm 51 produces for this mindset, verse 13. David firmly states that only after the process of the first 12 verses is he ready to "then" teach God's ways to sinners. He also clearly states the purpose, so that other people like himself will turn back to God. The most effective people in helping codependents find truth, hope, and restoration, are other codependents that have experienced these already. The other obvious condition is that the psalm is not finished; there is more to come in this process of internal cleansing.

David's prayer continues in verse 14, but adds a point of acceptance that is a lesson for codependents. He has already confessed his wrongs, prayed for cleansing, and desires forgiveness. But the language of this verse is addressing bloodshed, and the fact that no matter how much God could restore David; the shedding of Uriah's blood was a permanent and unchangeable fact. He had done something that could never be made right. He then points to God as his "Savior," and claims that deliverance from his guilt will result in songs of the Lord's righteousness. All codependents have done something they can never erase, either in word or deed that has caused harm to other people. But if they have come this far in the cleansing process, they can receive pardon from the Lord and find peace. This is what David is seeking: a pardon from God for the guilt is his bloodshed.

It could seem that verse 14 is an attempt to avoid responsibility, just to get a pardon from God and then everything is fine. But verse 15 is a request to speak and not remain silent. David goes as far as to ask the Lord to "open his lips," a statement that might indicate David needed help to speak. What this really means for codependents is that pardon comes with the responsibility to speak, even when they really don't want to. In other words, making amends for wrongs done. There are wrongs that can never be made right, but there are also wrongs that can be corrected. Recovery from codependency requires reconciliation, which is only possible when the lips of the codependent are opened to speak. David states the reason for speaking is to declare praise for God. Making amends is about declaring to another person what God has done in the life of the offender, and the desire to seek forgiveness. Whether the amends is received by the other party is irrelevant, codependents have to speak without expectation.

The next verse is somewhat of a disclaimer, where David states twice what God does not want from him. The references in verse 16 are to the established method of forgiveness for sins that was used in the Old Testament, where sacrifices and burnt offerings were brought to the temple. David says he is willing to bring them, but disqualifies them as not being what God wants. The application for codependents is that God is not looking for an external solution, one that involves deeds or following a set of rules to make God happy. This type of activity has been part of the problem, so it cannot be part of the solution. While this verse is really setting up the context of the next one, it is also removing the final barrier to the cleansing of the soul that has been the focus of this entire chapter. Any thought that a codependent can act good enough to earn God's love and forgiveness is cast aside. No religious rituals, no brownie points for being a good person. A common response by codependents when their sins are exposed is to quickly polish up their act. So, just in case any thought of putting on a good show remains, it is disqualified here.

Lastly, David confirms what God really wants as a sacrifice. The words "broken" and "contrite" actually mean the same thing, since contrite means to be broken or crushed. This relates back to verse eight where David speaks of crushed bones, but this time he specifically points to his spirit and his heart. The double use of the term is simply for the intensity of the statement, as if to say it is the best he can do. The end of the psalm is not a confession or a request; it is a statement of confidence. Throughout Psalm 51 David has been pouring out his heart in confessing his sins, and pleading with God for forgiveness and healing. He now ends by declaring that it is enough, that what he is bringing to God will not be rejected (despised), but will be accepted. For codependents to experience the soul cleansing and healing that comes from a solution like Psalm 51, there has to be a point at which it is enough. Striving for perfection is not the goal, neither is pleasing people or hiding from them. If the whole process has been followed, and the words of reconciliation have been spoken to other people, and the right attitude is maintained with God, then it is enough.

Summary of the Psalm 51 Solution

CONFESSION:
Accept your true condition without denial.
Seek God's mercy for cleansing and healing.
Believe that your guilt is ultimately against God.
Agree with God that the journey is inward, not outward.
Set aside any accomplishments from the past.
PRAYER:
Ask the Creator to give you a clean heart,
no matter what it takes.
Cry out to your Heavenly Father, for joy with pain.
Ask God to forgive you, for everything.
Trust that He will not abandon you.
Be confident that God will restore and sustain you.
ACTION:
Help others who struggle with the same problem.
Reconcile the wrongs you have done.
Speak when you need to speak.
Maintain the right attitude with God.
Finish the process.

For all codependents *The Third Option* is where God is ready to meet you. He wants to take you out of the extremes of life and give you a balance that works. For some this might be the first time they seek God; for others they have known Him in the past and left it all behind. Still others that have been in church all their lives will need to humbly and honestly admit their own condition, and realize that, despite their heritage or great accomplishments for God, they are spiritually sick and need healing.

"*If we claim to be without sin, we deceive ourselves and the truth is not in us. If we confess our sins, he is faithful and just and will forgive us our sins and purify us from all unrighteousness. If we claim we have not sinned, we make him out to be a liar and his word is not in us."* I John 1:8-10.

This scripture states that if we say we are without sin that the truth is not with us. It can come as a crushing blow when a person has to admit the truth, that their understanding of God which they believed was so strong was actually weak and needs to change. For mild codependents the experience does not have to be so intense, it can be the simple but powerful change to "let go and let God."

The Third Option relates to healing from codependency. Mild codependents who come to the point where they realize some of their decisions were not healthy and may be defined as enabling can experience pain with joy when they cry out to their Father in heaven, and receive his healing. People who are simply crushed by the truth remain defeated without the joy of the Lord. It is heart-breaking to see people who feel hopeless over the loss of a loved one and remain filled with guilt and shame. When there are only two options, avoiding the reality of the situation or being con-sumed by it, then healing will never come because of the condition of codependency. *The Third Option* is in the balance between the extremes, where pain and joy exist together.

Flaming codependents that experience the truth about the damage they have produced in the world must come the point where they realize who the problem is, and take an honest look at themselves. *"Partial acceptance is as worthless as partial truth."* Only full acceptance brings healing, even if it comes gradually as a person discovers more about themselves from peeling back the layers of denial. The process is halted or reversed when the truth is known but rejected. The extremes of denial, blame, and avoidance prevent the possibility of *The Third Option*.

Identifying and removing the obstacles has been the focus of this entire book. Whether it is denial of being codependent, living in the fog, or misconceptions about one of the many issues addressed, the solution lies in accepting the truth, seeking God, and making changes. It is a lifetime process. The only way to fail is to quit.

"For I am convinced that neither death nor life, neither angels nor demons, neither the present nor the future, nor any powers, neither height nor depth, nor anything else in all creation, will be able to separate us from the love of God that is in Christ Jesus our Lord." Romans 8:38-39

A Personal Note
For all that God has done in my life,
to mold and shape a spiritually sick person into a servant,
to trade the ashes of my sins for the beauty of His grace,
to touch my life with the anointing of His presence,
I am truly grateful, and responsible.

Isaiah 61:1-3
The Spirit of the Sovereign LORD is on me,
because the LORD has anointed me
to proclaim good news to the poor.
He has sent me to bind up the brokenhearted,
to proclaim freedom for the captives
and release from darkness for the prisoners,
to proclaim the year of the LORD's favor
and the day of vengeance of our God,
to comfort all who mourn,
and provide for those who grieve in Zion—
to bestow on them a crown of beauty instead of ashes,
the oil of joy instead of mourning,
and a garment of praise instead of a spirit of despair.

Are you ready to begin?

BIBLIOGRAPHY

Unless otherwise noted, scriptures are taken from the Holy Bible, New International Version, Zondervan Bible Publishers, Grand Rapids, MI, 1973, 1978, 1984.

BOOKS

Alchoholics Anonymous "Big Book" 4th Edition, Alcoholics Anonymous World Services, Inc., New York, NY, 2001.

Beattie, Melody, *Codependent No More* (Harper/Hazelden, New York, NY, 1987).

Bradshaw, John, *Healing the Shame That Binds You* (Health Communications, Inc., Deerfield, FL., 1988).

Cloud, Henry & Townsend, John, *Boundaries* (Zondervan, Grand Rapids, MI, 1992).

Doninger, Wendy, *On Hinduism* (Oxford University Press, New York, NY, 2014).

Horne, Steve, *7 Things Christians Need to Know About Addictions* (Heritage Builders Publishing, Monterey, CA, 2016).

One Day At A Time, Al-anon Family Group Headquarters, Inc. New York, NY, 1988.

Strong, James S.T.D, LL.D, Strong's Exhaustive Concordance (World Bible Publishers, Iowa Falls, Iowa, 1986).

Woititz, Janet Geringer, Adult Children of Alcoholics (Health Communications, Inc., Deerfield, FL, 1990.

PAMPHLETS

Lerner, Rokelle, *Boundaries for Codependents* (Hazelden, Center City, MN, 1988).

WORKBOOKS

Christian Adults in Recovery, Maki, Julianne & Maki, Mark (Brea, CA, 1992)
Wilderness Quest, (Moab, UT)

TELEVISION

Healing the Shame that Binds You, Bradshaw, John (one-hour program, 1987 on PBS)
Intervention, Mettler, Sam (A&E Networks, New York, NY, 2005-2015)

RADIO/AUDIO

Earll, Bob (Robert). A.A. Circuit Speaker. Audio recording, pre-1996.
Focus on the Family, Dobson, James (Daily Worldwide Radio Program, Colorado Springs, CO, 1997-2017).

MOVIES

Forrest Gump- Roth, Eric (Paramount Pictures, Hollywood, CA, 1994).
The Fog – Carpenter, John (MGM, Beverly Hills, CA, 1980).
The Sandlot – Evans, David & Gunter, Robert (20th Century Fox, Glendale, CA, 1993).

MUSIC

Lee, Johnny – *Looking for Love* (Full Moon Records, New York, NY, 1980).
Wynette, Tammy – *Stand By Your Man* (Columbia Recording Studios, Nashville, TN, 1968)

WEBSITES

Bible Hub Website (*Various Concordances, Bible Translations, Commentaries*). http://biblehub.com

Britannica. https://www.britannica.com

Bureau of Prisons (2015, July 17) *Percentage of inmates for crimes related to addiction.*

Google Search 2017, *Definition of Validation*, http://www.google.com/#q=definition+of+validation

Loria, Joe (2017, April 20). *You Can't Eat Meat and Be an Environmentalist. Period.* Retrieved from Mercy for Animals, http://www.mercyforanimals.org

Marrying Pets, http://marryyourpet.com

NOAA National Severe Storms Laboratory, Norman, OK. http://www.nssl.noaa.gov/

Westheimer, Ruth (*Dr. Ruth*) http://www.drruth.com

Wikipeida. https://en.wikipedia.org

AUTHOR'S ORIGINAL WRITINGS
(in order by date)

Horne, Steve.

Freedom From Abandonment. Written, Audio, and Video. 1999 (includes the Dialogue of Addiction)

Reconciliation. Written & Video. 2000 (Validation Cards)

Healing a Broken Spirit Series – Part 3: Secondary Addictions. Written (English 2000 & Russian 2006).

Out of More Extremes Series – Part 4: Family of Origin: Written & Audio. 2002

Out of More Extremes Series – Part 6: Self Esteem: Written & Audio. 2002

Steps of Courage Series – Part 2: Codependency. Written & Audio. 2002.

Steps of Courage Series – Part 3: Grief. Written & Audio. 2002.

Out of Emotional Extremes Series – Part 1: Shame. Written & Audio. 2003 (Circle of Identity Diagram)

Out of Emotional Extremes Series – Part 2: Guilt. Written & Audio. 2003

Worship the Creator Series – Part 5: The Secret of Sin. Written (English 2005 & Russian 2006).

Anger Series – Part 6: The Sin of Offence. Written (English & Russian). 2008.
Book of James Series – Chapter 2 Part 1: Killer Poodles. Written. 2009.
Family Support Group – Part 2: Codependency. Written. 2010
Christian Recovery 101 Series – Part 4: Dependence. Written. 2011
The Most Codependent Woman in the Bible: The Samaritan Woman.
Written & Video. 2012.

RECOVERY COMMON STATEMENTS & CLICHÉ'S
(Source Unknown)

"Doing the same thing over and over and expecting a different result
(definition of insanity)."
"Recovery will ruin your drinking."
"Old Tapes." (reference to internal thoughts).
"Fight or Flight."
"Look at all that I do for you and this is the thanks I get."
"You must surrender to win."
"Gossiping is talking about a person when you are not part of the prob-
lem or the solution."
Other common statements and cliché's used whose source is unknown.

CPSIA information can be obtained
at www.ICGtesting.com
Printed in the USA
LVHW052006110419
613841LV00002B/2